Writing

THE SEA

Library and Archives Canada Cataloguing in Publication

Brown, Cassie, 1919-1986.
Writing the sea / Cassie Brown.

ISBN 1-894463-74-9

1. Shipwrecks--Newfoundland. I. Title.

FC2170.S5B765 2005   910'.9163'44   C2005-903307-X

PRINTED IN CANADA

Cover photo: Brian Bursey

FLANKER PRESS LTD.
ST. JOHN'S, NL, CANADA
TOLL FREE: 1-866-739-4420
WWW.FLANKERPRESS.COM

Canada

We acknowledge the financial support of the Government of Canada through the
Book Publishing Industry Development Program (BPIDP) for our publishing program.

Canada Council   Conseil des Arts
for the Arts   du Canada

We acknowledge the support of the Canada Council for the Arts
which last year invested $20.3 million in writing and publishing throughout Canada.

We acknowledge financial support from the Government of Newfoundland
and Labrador, Department of Tourism, Culture and Recreation.

Writing
THE SEA

CASSIE BROWN

FLANKER PRESS LTD.
ST. JOHN'S, NL
2005

TABLE OF CONTENTS

Photographs

All the photographs in this work are from the Cassie Brown Collection, Centre for Newfoundland Studies Archives, Memorial University of Newfoundland, St. John's, Newfoundland, Canada.

Acknowledgements

The publisher wishes to thank Bert Riggs and Gail Weir of the staff at the Centre for Newfoundland Studies Archives, Memorial University, St. John's, Newfoundland, for their assistance in researching the material and photographs for this book.

In addition, a debt of gratitude is owed to Mr. John Zeggil of the Toronto-Dominion Bank, St. John's, Newfoundland.

The publisher is also indebted to Vera McDonald for her research and editorial assistance. Thanks also go to the Cranfords—Margo, Justin, and Jerry—for their assistance in editorial, design, and technical contributions.

FOREWORD

Writing the Sea includes those short stories previously published in the book *The Caribou Disaster and Other Short Stories*, a collection of articles and features from the pages of the St. John's daily newspaper *The Daily News*, written in the period 1959–1966, when Ms. Brown worked as a reporter and, later, as women's editor.

New to this volume are two major additions. "Rose Blanche and Me" is an autobiographical essay written by Cassie Brown for Joseph R. Smallwood's *Encyclopedia of Newfoundland and Labrador*. The second major addition is an edited transcript of a question-and-answer session, conducted by long-distance, between Cassie and students of G.C. Rowe Junior High School, Corner Brook, Newfoundland, and co-ordinated by teacher Floyd Spracklin.

The stories should be read in the context of the time frame in which they were written and the newspaper environment — with deadlines! As such, they read somewhat unevenly. Several items required little time and effort to complete, needing only one short interview, and were written straightforwardly, in the voice of a reporter. For example, "The Loss of the *Hope*."

Other articles were written as special features, requiring much more background research and multiple interviews for details and are written in the voice of the storyteller. An example of this is "Death March."

"Death March" was written as a special feature commemorating the fiftieth anniversary of the SS *Newfoundland* disaster, and the newspaper, realizing the significance of the event, permitted the writer to devote considerable time in conducting the research, writing, and editing. As a result, the final article was much more polished. The events and the graphic human tragedy arising from this sealing catastrophe so troubled Cassie Brown that she felt compelled to research and write the complete story. To do it justice, she eventually quit her salaried position as an editor at *The Daily News* and devoted her full time to the story, which developed as her signature piece, the best-selling *Death On The Ice*, one of the most widely read books in Newfoundland literature.

Another piece the author wrote for *The Daily News* was the story of the *Florizel* disaster on Newfoundland's Southern Shore, which she also developed into another best-selling book, titled *A Winter's Tale*.

Garry Cranford
Publisher

Rose Blanche and Me

ROARO

IT WAS AN INGLORIOUS NICKNAME, but from the first breath of life, my family says, I opened my mouth and yelled bloody murder. Whatever the cause, I kicked up racket enough to wake the dead and carried out in like manner through the first few years of existence, thus earning the ignominious nickname of "Roaro."

Cassie Brown at eight years old.

Day and night the windswept hills of Rose Blanche reverberated with the cries of the crossest baby that was ever born. One summer day in my second year as I was developing even greater lung power and sending piercing shrieks into the firmament, my grandmother

1

Horwood surveyed me with a glitter in her eye and stated, "It's that curly hair; that's what's making her so cross." (I had a head of bouncing golden curls.)

My grandmother was steeped in folklore. My mother, a former schoolteacher, was not. "Oh, I don't think that has anything to do with it," she demurred, and that was very brave of her, because my grandmother was not a lady to tangle with.

"I am sure it is," Granny said firmly, with all the reasonable logic of a woman who brooks no argument.

"What have curls got to do with it?" my mother was so bold as to ask.

"All curly-headed children are cross children," Grandmother stated. "Cut off her curls and she will be a good, quiet little girl."

Let me state categorically that one did not argue with my grandmother; when she gave an opinion you did not seek to change the subject, and discussion of my curls and subsequent crossness was dropped.

A few days later, as the hills were reverberating with the sound of my unmusical carolling, Granny swooped down on me and carted me, still howling, to the privacy of her own home, where she snipped each and every curl from my head. To her delight and justification the big scissors — the snipping sound — shocked me into silence.

"There!" she said triumphantly, planting shorn little me, still in a state of shocked silence, in my mother's arms. "You'll find she won't be cross from now on."

Alas! It did not curb my tendency to yell bloody murder at the drop of a hat. If anything, the loss of my curls seemed to have enraged me further, though how I dared to act contrary to my grandmother's expectations can only be put down to my extreme youthfulness and lack of understanding that Grandmother was always right.

I was still embarrassed by the name "Roaro," which had clung to me until I started school, and I truly never understood why such a name had been tacked on to me. You see, somewhere along the way I had become a tractable, quiet, obedient, and dutiful child. I made no unnecessary noise. I did not rock the boat.

I was simply there.

My grandmother was a living contradiction; loving, kind, the most generous of persons, she was also cruel, a tartar whose tongue lashed you mercilessly if you were caught in a misdemeanour. You stood by helplessly before her, flayed and shrivelled as the acid dripped from her tongue and forever scarred your inner soul; then, before you could crawl away to lick your wounds, you were marched into her house, plunked at her table, and your self-esteem restored with the most delectable goodies for which she was rightly famous.

She was, in truth, an astonishing woman. The reigning queen of Rose Blanche, the matriarch, the supreme commander, and her word was law. To me she was bigger than any other woman in the world, and my tongue clove to the roof of my mouth if she addressed me in anger.

I loved her beans and was privileged to sit at her table every Wednesday for supper, and they were always the same—perfect.

At Christmas we were allowed into her dining room and parlour. My father would play the organ, and in her turn Granny would play the gramophone;

and we were allowed to listen to the glorious voice of Galli Kurchi (or was it Marion Talley?) singing "The Holy City." Mind you, we also listened to Jimmy Rogers singing "Waiting for a Train," but it was our delight to listen to Granny sing along with Galli Kurchi (or Marion Talley or whoever). She did it for fun, and we tittered dutifully, but her voice was as pure and as golden as Miss Kurchi's. High, true, and faultless, and if I had the courage of a lion I would have told her so.

I did not, though. Children were seen and not heard; it would have been highly presumptuous of me to venture any opinion.

I liked my grandmother.

I did not have the courage not to.

Children should be seen and not heard.

I grew up with that philosophy dinned in my ears. My parents did not know any different because they had grown up with the same philosophy, and they believed it. I believed it. I did not engage in idle chatter, but I did a lot of thinking, I can tell you. I had become the good, quiet little girl my granny had predicted I would become, and my hair was now brown and as straight as a whip.

Just the same, there was a stubborn streak that dared to emerge now and then.

The schoolhouse in Rose Blanche had two classrooms and a concert hall. The female, lower-grade teacher and the male principal were alien creatures, stern and forbidding. To be singled out for questioning turned my brain to jelly.

I obediently tried to absorb all they shoved in my direction but do not recall being outstandingly brilliant. Once, the principal stood the whole grade in a line for spelling and, to my embarrassment, I found myself at the top of the class, being the only one who could spell Labrador.

It was the only time I recall being at the top of the class.

The principal was a cold, stern man who did not believe in "sparing the rod," a hefty broomstick in this case, which he used frequently and with great enjoyment, but on the boys only. Nevertheless, when I did not know my lessons well I contemplated running away from home, only there was no place to run.

One winter a boy let it be known to the school at large that he liked me very much, and continually pelted me with snowballs. In the eyes of the schoolchildren he became my boyfriend, though in truth I do not recall ever speaking to him.

Though it behooved me to pretend he did not exist, I secretly delighted at being pelted with snowballs.

We had a "jiggly bridge" (suspension bridge, to you) in Rose Blanche. It was suspended over the tumbling waters of Rose Blanche Brook in Diamond Cove, and in summer it was the Sunday meeting place of all the young people, even the smaller ones like me. The boys would lure the girls on to the bridge, then, taking fiendish delight in jumping up and down, cause the bridge to undulate alarmingly. The bigger girls, knowing what to expect, hung on to the cables and screamed to keep the boys happy.

Being of a rather timid nature I was a little more cautious and usually tried to cross Jiggly Bridge when the boys were more interested in watching the salmon hurtle up over the small waterfalls.

Actually, Jiggly Bridge made me seasick. My muscles had a tendency to seize up the moment I felt the boards buckle and sway beneath my feet. To get from one side to the other was a terrifying adventure for a small girl: one staggered, lurched, and bounced across the undulating, careening boards, and how or why I never pitched through the cables to the rushing water below is beyond me.

Once, I did get caught right in the middle. The boys jumped up and down until the bridge was about turning upside down, swaying and buckling in the most terrifying manner. I remember falling on my knees, yelling bloody murder, and hanging on like grim death to the cables while everyone shrieked with laughter.

I was the only one who did not think it was funny.

Whatever the dynamics involved in the building of suspension bridges, I find it rather astonishing in retrospect that one should have been built in isolated Rose Blanche, considering the fact that a mere half a dozen families (or less) lived on the other side of the brook. Regrettably, it no longer exists, having been torn down to make way for a very prosaic concrete bridge to accommodate motor traffic.

FATHER MESSIAH

ROSE BLANCHE ANGLICAN CHURCH was a small white wooden structure with a steeple, and stained glass windows over the altar. Rose Blanche people sat in the pews on the right aisle. Harbour le Cou people sat in the pews on the left aisle—and couldn't they sing!

Our pew was the fifth from the front on the right aisle, and we went to church every Sunday morning and evening, sometimes with Father, sometimes with Grandfather. I have no recollection, ever, of seeing my mother or grandmother in church (but that is only my recollection).

The choir was very small, and I do not remember hearing any hymns sung in harmony, but my father more than made up for lack of choral harmony. In his deep voice he sang bass from our pew and was the most distinctive singer in the whole congregation.

My father, Wilson, was nonconformist, of course, an individual who did pretty well what he wanted to do, and it amused him to see the surreptitious looks cast his way. He was spoiled rotten by my grandfather, my grandmother, by the whole community for that matter, and if he wanted to do handsprings in the church it is doubtful if anyone would have said "Boo!"

Being of a rather timid and unobtrusive tempera-ment myself, I, too, kept throwing surreptitious looks at my father and wondered privately if his singing was the reason why my mother never went to church.

Once, a great Anglican priest came to visit us in Rose Blanche. His name was Father Messiah, and I thought he was God.

We had all been preached at about Jesus the Messiah, and the Bible teaches that Jesus was the Son of God. Jesus and God were one and the same, in some intangible sort of way. It was all very confusing, and I did not think too much about it, because, it seemed to me, nobody knew what they were talking about, not until I saw Father Messiah.

Nobody had said he was God, mind you, but we had to line up at the wharf and wave flags and everything when he landed. But when I saw him—tall, old, with benevolent eyes and noble mien and giving us his blessing—it came to me suddenly that He was God. After all, his name was Messiah and he looked very much like the drawings of the holy men we had seen in the Bible, so the whole thing fell neatly into place. Even though he didn't look like the picture of Jesus the Messiah, it was his name and he did look like what we thought God looked like.

I was quite sure he was God.

CARLO

WE ALWAYS HAD A BIG BONFIRE on November 5 each year. Old barrels, scrub, anything that would burn was hoarded, and for weeks in advance everybody was stealing everybody else's old barrels to see who could have the biggest bonfire.

We didn't call it Guy Fawkes Day. It was simply Bonfire Day, and my young sister, Freda, whose birthday was November 5, grew up firmly believing that Bonfire Day was strictly in observance of her birthday.

Carlo and I never did get along well.

He was such a big Newfoundland dog. He could gobble me up in one snap, which is what he had in mind, I am sure.

The trouble, Carlo was not as gentle and amiable as most Newfoundland dogs are reputed to be. If anything, he was a great bully of a dog who stalked among us children, bowling us aside like ninepins and generally getting his kicks when we ran screaming to Mother. Was he docile and loving like the average Newfoundland dog? Did he beg to be mauled and petted by loving children, like all Newfoundland dogs? Was he the big hero as all Newfoundland dogs are reputed to be, eager and panting to save the life of anyone in danger of drowning?

Not on your life.

When he sent us screaming he leered and sneered, then looked slyly innocent and naive, as if butter wouldn't melt in his mouth.

If I approached him for a timid, friendly pat, he growled softly and it was clear to me that he was saying, "Beat it. Don't bother me."

When I fell overboard in twenty-five feet of ocean, was Carlo there, panting and eager to save my life?

He was not!

And *this* dog was the pride of my father's brood of Newfoundland dogs. This surly, ungracious, deceitful dog, who could look as if he would lay down his life for you, was the big wheel, the kingpin in the family brood. Whatever his qualifications were for breeding purposes, he was in great demand and I can only assume it had gone to his head.

Anyway, there was antipathy between the two of us, and the situation did not improve with time. My timidity and a propensity for introspection made me a fairly inconspicuous member of the family, and Carlo knew. I did not have the ability to convince my father that he was harbouring a viper in his nest. It was strictly between the two of us.

One sunny Sunday my father decided to take some pictures. Being a good amateur photographer, he frequently took family pictures. Today we children were to pose with Carlo, and my father decided that I should cuddle up close to Carlo. "Put your arm around his neck," he ordered.

Like a great, benign giant, Carlo was sitting obediently on the lawn, sending waves of hostility and contempt in my direction. "You dare," his attitude said to me.

I looked at my father and squeaked, "I'm afraid of Carlo."

"What?" my father cried in astonishment. "Afraid of Carlo? What nonsense, Daughter." Then he ordered, "Put your arm around his neck."

I was, above all, an obedient and dutiful child, so I knelt on the lawn and inched reluctantly toward Carlo. He didn't move, but his brown eye swivelled in my direction, and his attitude said, quite unmistakably, "I dare you."

I was caught between my father and the dog. To disobey my father was unheard of, to disobey Carlo's clear warning was suicide. What to do?

For a brief moment I pictured myself a free soul with the courage of a lion telling my father that he could not make me do these things that I did not want to do, but the spark died aborning when my father's voice rose impatiently, "Daughter!"

I inched closer to Carlo, sending waves of fear. He reacted with a definite growl.

I stopped, nailed to the ground. I did not have the courage to disobey my father.

With the wind fluffing his rusty black coat, the personification of docility and serenity, Carlo sat nobly, only poor me able to see the evil in his eye. My father, on the other hand, was becoming annoyed. He expected implicit obedience to his every command. "Do as I tell you, Daughter," he said with ominous calm.

I did not move. In fact, I dared to scowl. A surge of stubbornness rose fiercely inside me, and none was more surprise at this than I. My father looked long and hard at me, ignoring my sisters and brothers who were fidgeting restlessly.

I squinted back, not knowing what to expect. Death, perhaps.

I was saved only by a noisy, rambunctious little sister Freda, who ignored my father's commands as if they were unimportant, nothing words. She had lost interest in having her picture taken and began to wander off. My father hastily put her back, ignored me, and snapped the picture.

I still have that snapshot. Carlo looks noble, lovable, a darling. I look surly and ungracious — a child only a mother could love.

DROWNING: OVER THE SLIPWAY

About that falling overboard. I still vividly remember the frightening sensation of drowning, of fighting for air, that ghastly, smothering feeling that you're dying.

I had no business being where I was, of course. Our orders had been most explicit—stay away from the wharf. But even the most obedient and dutiful child could not resist the sweet whisperings of the sea. It sang me to sleep at night, it woke me in the mornings. It had woven itself into the fibres of my being and I was drawn like a magnet because it whispered soft and lovely things to me.

To my mother it was a constant threat to her brood, and she forbade us the wharf where big steamers and small steamers used to come every so often.

On this day I plotted my course deviously, playing on the big rocks surrounding our house, but edging away until I could have seemingly, innocently, played myself right to the wharf and out of my mother's sight.

There were fishermen on the wharf, all busily cleaning fish and taking no notice of me, so I ducked down the slipway that ran out over the sea and lay flat on my stomach to stare into the icy green depths at the connors darting here and there.

Being most generally a very obedient child, great waves of guilt were doing strange things to my conscience, and to assuage them I thought I would clean the slipway, which reeked of fish. With the best intentions in the world I picked up a great fish broom, dipped it into the sea where it lapped over the slipway, and began to sweep vigorously.

I swept myself overboard into twenty-five feet of water.

What I remember mostly was the struggle for air, and the size of the wharf posts. They were enormous.

It registered on one part of my brain that the wharf posts were *really* enormous, like giant columns, and dimly it surprised me that I hadn't noticed before just how enormous they were. "It must be a really big wharf," one part of my mind said in astonishment as I kicked, splashed, and took water into my lungs and stomach.

As I strangled and choked for air and was disappearing under water for the last time, a hand closed around my ankle and, with the touch of human hands on me, I was suddenly able to breathe.

The dangerous waters near the Rose Blanche lighthouse.

It was later explained to me that my struggles had taken me well out from the slipway and not one of the fishermen on the wharf could swim. But the alarm went up, and our storekeeper, a young man by the name of Charlie Newman, had come flying to the wharf. He couldn't swim either, but, holding hands, he and the fishermen formed a human lifeline with Charlie in the lead, flinging themselves into the sea, reaching me as I was sinking, exhausted, for the third time to the bottom.

I don't recall ever saying "thank you" to Charlie and those other unknown fishermen, but I suspect my parents made me do so when I recovered from the shock.

Viewing them later, the wharf posts did not seem to be quite so enormous.

DROWNING: THROUGH THE ICE

I LOVED THE SEA AND IT LOVED ME, TOO. I know this because it kept trying to take me with it. My second narrow squeak came in the dead of winter when the ice was a good two feet thick on the harbour.

We had a maid, you see. I don't remember her name or anything, except that she was young and she "lived in." One frosty Sunday afternoon she and her best friend were going for a walk, towing me along between them. The harbour was frozen solid, but here and there holes had been sawn through the ice, for what purpose I do not know, but my companions had decided to cross the harbour.

When we got out there, smack in the middle, the two girls got into an argument about which way to go. One wished to visit relatives on Caines Island in the mouth of the harbour while the other wished to go to Misery Point, a picturesque part of Rose Blanche with houses perched on bare rock. Anyway, I distinctly remember the two girls arguing, not angrily, mind you, but they were not looking where they were going and did not see the large, round hole in the ice.

My next recollection is me up to my neck in the briny, staring at the green-tinted ice. The girl on my right had her left leg in the hole, the girl on my left had her right leg in the hole. Both had the foresight to hang on to me.

I do not remember the mad dash across the ice to home with my clothes freezing around my body. My recollection ends with me up to my neck in the harbour staring at the green-tinted ice.

DROWNING: GARIA BAY

My PARENTS, BEING BUSINESS PEOPLE, had a great social life. Our home was open to any visitor who arrived in Rose Blanche. My mother had to be prepared at all times for any number of people who might drop in. Between her and my grandmother, they could have serviced a delicatessen.

Farmer's Brook and Garia Bay a few miles down the coast were famous for salmon fishing, and any American notable who came our way invariably would end up under our roof. There was Zane Grey, novelist, whom I do not personally remember except through hearsay, and an American millionaire by the name of Dickinson, who had his own big white yacht skippered by a Newfoundland crew. I do not remember Mr. Dickinson either, but I do remember the big white yacht.

Once, we had some very illustrious relatives visiting us from St. John's, on the other end of the island, and some from Sydney, Nova Scotia, Canada. I guess you could call it a family reunion. Anyway, wishing to impress the sophisticated relatives from the big cities, my father wired his friend, Mr. Dickinson, asking for the use of his yacht for a weekend of fishing in Garia Bay. On Friday morning the yacht steamed into Rose Blanche harbour, all flags fluttering, and the whole Horwood clan, plus several good friends including the good doctor and his wife, steamed out of Rose Blanche for an unforgettable weekend.

They had a ball, and I got seasick. The doctor split the seat of his pants and had to wear a dried codfish to cover the gap. The city relatives were utterly bedazzled by the stunning scenery of Garia Bay, and I thought I was dying.

The party continued on into the night when we were at anchor. It was a placid night, with a big moon hanging over the bay, and so breathtakingly beautiful that I still have a time trying to convince myself it was real. But I'll tell you this: the quiet and tranquility of Garia Bay really took a beating that Friday night.

My mother caught her first salmon on this trip, and again I nearly drowned.

Saturday morning was brilliantly sunny. The family were not inclined to lie around, because they took their salmon fishing seriously. My father and mother, giving my sister Vera and me orders to follow, began to traipse upriver. They were equipped with hip rubbers and all of the fishing paraphernalia. Vera and I wore our second Sunday best. I was wearing new shoes.

Actually, we would much rather have stayed behind and played with the other children who were permitted to explore along the shoreline of Garia Bay. We could hear their delighted shouts of laughter as they skipped rocks into the bay and such.

Those delightful sounds faded as we reluctantly trailed behind Father and Mother, silently rebellious at having to go with the "old" people.

Garia River was wide and shallow, overhung in areas with brambles of delicious wild berries, and my resentment disappeared as we had our fill while our parents fished. It was idyllic, really. The river sang and danced by, the green hills were so fresh and clean, the birds serenaded us, laying a cloak of tranquility over my smouldering resentment. I was peaceful and happy by the time my parents decided to cross the river in order to fish on the sweeping curve of the river bend.

My father went first, followed by my mother, the water creaming up over their shins. My sister and I, wearing only our shoes, stayed indecisively on the bank. My father, noting that we had not followed, ordered, "Come along, Daughters."

Vera obediently plunged into the river, shoes and all, and sloshed to my father's side. My mother was already moving upstream.

Still I hesitated. I was wearing new shoes, and one did not lightly ruin new shoes, or anything new for that matter, so I just stood there in an agony of indecision.

My father's voice bellowed across the rushing waters: "Cassie!"

I pointed to my new shoes and squeaked, "My new shoes..."

He roared impatiently, "Come along!"

With much trepidation and uncertainty I plunged up to my knees in the rushing river.

Whereas my sister had ploughed boldly onward and reached the opposite bank without mishap, my timid movements were causing problems. My shoes were slipping on the rocks, and with each uncertain step the river was threatening to tumble me head over heels.

"Hurry!" my father commanded.

I hurried and stepped into a hole.

It was not a very deep hole, but it did the trick, tumbling me into the river where I flailed and kicked to no avail. The rushing waters pinned me to the hole and I was again under water and drowning, taking great gulps of water into my lungs and stomach. Each gasp, each snort for air, brought water inside me.

Above the rush of the river above my head I heard my father's annoyed bellow, "Get up!"

I did not care to increase my father's wrath, so I stopped drowning and got up.

Very shortly afterward my mother caught her first salmon, of which we were all inordinately proud.

Everybody had a wonderful time. Saturday night the hills of Garia Bay rang to the shouts and merriment of our party, and the city people were terribly impressed by the weekend on the millionaire's yacht, and the family reunion was a success beyond their wildest dreams.

In 1929 this same millionaire (so it came to us), joined the hordes of other millionaires who had lost their fortune in the Great Depression, and jumped from a window.

ANTIDOTE TO DROWNING

ONE SUNNY SUNDAY, as we were picnicking in Diamond Cove, near Jiggly Bridge, my father and I had a confrontation.

He was swimming in the icy ocean and exulting in it. I and my sisters and brothers had been coerced into swimming suits but found the Arctic chill of the sea too much.

"Come along, Daughter," said my father, and I obediently approached the sea's edge, where I halted.

"You'll love it," he coaxed, and held out his arms. "Come on."

I stuck the minutest piece of flesh of my big toe into the water and turned into petrified rock. My teeth chattered and goosebumps stuck out all over me and no movement came to my paralyzed limbs.

My father's voice grew very firm. "Cassie, I am going to teach you how to swim. Come here!"

Goodness knows I was sick and tired of near drownings, but to deliberately walk into the Arctic chill of the ocean was beyond my physical capabilities. Besides, the concentrated attention of my father was a terrifying prospect. It was too much.

I stood there quaking with the cold, and my father surged toward me.

My feet suddenly developed wings and I fled, away from the beach, across the little road, and up into the woods.

"Daughter, come back here," my father roared.

But I would not. I hid there until the flies drove me out. My father was still floating in the sea and having a wonderful time, and he never did get around to teaching me how to swim, thank goodness.

I taught myself to swim a few years later.

STOWING AWAY
ON THE *APHRODITE*

THE *APHRODITE* WAS EVERYTHING her name implied: a beautiful, gracious, three-masted Danish ship, spanking shining clean, all polished hardwood and gleaming brass, complete with storybook captains and crew, all handsome, blond, and blue-eyed sailormen. Captain Watson was more grey than blond and he was a little portly, but he had the Old World courtesy which charmed men, women, and children. He spent much time in the homes of my parents, grandparents, and my aunt. We all adored this.

The *Aphrodite* arrived from Oporto, Portugal, every summer and filled her holds with our salt cod. Being a thing of beauty and a joy to behold, she drew wistful looks from the young would-be sailors of Rose Blanche. They hung around her in dories and had their first love affair with a beautiful ship.

It was on the *Aphrodite* that I finally ran away from home.

I have no recollection of the cause, but it must have been for all those unfulfilled moments of silent rebellion. The instigator may have been my cousin, Billy Rolls, a spirited, wilful boy around my age who must have had a difference of opinion with one or both of his parents. It is not clear to me now how or why it all came about, but this recollection starts with the two of us, each carrying a minuscule amount of clothing tied in a white cloth, crouched in a locker on the deck of the ship. How we actually got aboard and hid ourselves on a ship swarming with sailors is something I cannot figure out, but Billy and I actually hid in the locker, determined to run away to Oporto, Portugal, with Captain Watson.

Relatives of Author Cassie Brown visit the Rose Blanche lighthouse. L-R: Margo Cranford, Vera McDonald, and Harriett Hardy.

My next recollection is sitting in Captain Watson's gleaming cabin eating delicious figs, sugared jellies and the like, and being generally treated like royalty, but I was feeling just a little bit seasick. My cousin was terribly excited about going to Portugal, but what my thoughts were on the subject I cannot recall.

We were, at this time, outside Rose Blanche harbour, and the next thing we knew all the motorboats were converging on the *Aphrodite* and my father and uncle and millions of others were clustered around the ship to take us back home. I do not recall if we went gladly or sadly, but on the way back I got violently seasick.

Captain Watson courteously told Billy and me that if we wanted to go to Portugal next year, just let him know.

We said we would.

But we never did.

AN OLD FRIEND

THERE WAS THIS OLD, old woman who lived in an old, decrepit house right on the road, and every day she sat in the window and watched the world go by. She was frail and wispy and a little scary, although I wasn't really scared of her because I never saw her move from her window.

One day I was walking along the road with a big juicy orange in my hand and she tapped on the window, beckoning to me. I was so terrified my feet grew roots into the ground, but she kept beckoning and grimacing, and, being a very obedient child, I willed my feet to move and hauled myself to her door, wondering why the old woman wanted me.

Was she going to eat me?

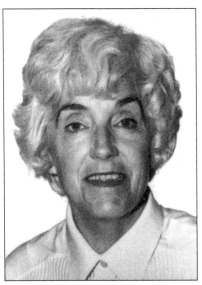

Cassie Brown in later years.

She came to the door, a frail, hunched old lady, and invited me inside her dark and dingy little kitchen. Everything smelled old and decaying and further terrified my timid soul.

She had no teeth and I never understood what she was saying, but she was pointing to the big juicy orange clutched in my hand. Mutely I gave it to her and watched silently as, with exquisite delicacy, her thin, gnarled fingers peeled the orange. With great care she broke the orange in half, kept one half for herself, and placed the other half in my paralyzed, upturned hand.

My recollection of the old lady and the orange ends there.

I loved Rose Blanche and mourned for a year when we moved to St. John's. Five or six years later, four of us returned to spend the whole summer with Granny and Dee and her family, and we discovered we were outsiders.

But I still go back.

The CARIBOU *Disaster*

OCTOBER 14, 1942

It was wartime and the SS *Caribou* was steaming steadily across the Gulf of St. Lawrence in the early hours of a cold fall morning. At 3:10 A.M. Newfoundland time, a torpedo from the 500-ton German U-boat *U-69* hit the *Caribou* amidships on the starboard side, and within minutes she sank, taking with her men, women, and children. She went down in the deepest channel in the Gulf, twenty-five miles southwest of Channel Head in the vicinity of St. Paul's Island.

It was a bright night, too bright to suit Captain Ben Tavenor, according to Thomas Fleming, who was the purser on the *Caribou*. He had a premonition that something was about to happen, and he voiced those fears to Mr. Fleming only two hours before disaster struck.

Another passenger, William J. Lundrigan of Corner Brook, also had the feeling of impending disaster. From the moment he stepped on board the *Caribou* at North Sydney, he couldn't shake the feeling that the ship was doomed.

P/O Gerald Bastow, a young airman who had just finished a Fighter Operational Training Course, was coming home on embarkation leave before proceeding to the United Kingdom for operation duty with the Royal Air Force, and he boarded the *Caribou* with his friends, P/O Bob Butt and Edgar Martin. Gerald Bastow also had a premonition of disaster.

The launch of the SS *Caribou* at Rotterdam in the Netherlands in July of 1925.

He and his friends spent several hours on deck and in the smoking saloon before retiring. While he and Bob Butt had finished their training course together, and were coming home together, they had waited over in Montreal a few days for Edgar Martin, a school friend of Gerald's, who had just graduated from McGill University with a B.Sc. degree.

Being military personnel, Gerald and Bob were embarked first and given their quarters, while Edgar boarded later and was quartered in another cabin.

Thomas Fleming had no time to think of danger. As the purser he was quite busy, for there were many women and children to be bedded down, and some of them had no sleeping accommodations. Many men gave up their berths to the women and children and made do in the saloon and the lounge.

At 1:00 A.M. he and his assistant, William Hogan of Carbonear, were in their office in the radio room on the bridge deck getting their papers ready for the early morning docking, when Captain Ben Tavenor walked in. He was restless and uneasy because they had only one escort ship and he didn't like the course they were steering, although it was a course set by the Royal Canadian Navy.

Captain Tavenor invited Tom to stroll around the deck with him, and as they walked he voiced the opinion that subs were lurking in the area where they were headed, around St. Paul's Island. "On a night like this, our smoke can be seen for miles," he said.

When he left Fleming, it was around 1:30 A.M. and Thomas went back to finish his paperwork. It was about two-thirty when they finished, and he and young Hogan lay on the two berths in their office to catch forty winks.

Charles Moores, a ticket agent for the Newfoundland Railway, was another uneasy passenger. He remained awake and fully clothed for the better part of the night ready for disaster. Finally, as the *Caribou* neared the Newfoundland coast, he did undress and lie down.

William J. Lundrigan was a sick man. He had recently developed a heart condition and had been told by his doctors that he needed a prolonged rest, and he was going home to Corner Brook to get that rest. But as he stepped aboard the *Caribou* the premonition of danger was very strong, and would remain with him.

He gave up his berth to a woman and was given a place to sleep in the lounge, but he could not rest or sleep.

All through the night he walked on the deck with people he knew, and with each passing hour the premonition of danger became stronger. Finally, when everyone else had gone to bed, he decided to familiarize himself with the part of the ship he would have to go to in case she was torpedoed.

He did so, finding the boat assigned to passengers in his section, and then he tried to sleep. But sleep would not come, and he rose again, retraced his steps to the boat and rechecked everything before going back to the lounge. Still the feeling of danger persisted, and he rose, altogether four times, and traced his way to the lifeboat before he eventually went to sleep, around 3:00 A.M.

It was 3:10 A.M. Newfoundland time when the torpedo struck, and in less than ten minutes the *Caribou* had gone under, taking with her Captain Ben Tavenor and his two sons, Stanley and Harold, most of the women and children who were below, and over half the people who were on her.

As he had rehearsed so many times earlier, William Lundrigan made his way to the lifeboat without any difficulty and discovered the ship was heeling over and going under fast. There was some difficulty getting the boat free, but she was eventually let down with nobody aboard, and all had to leap. William Lundrigan made it safely, though shaken and bruised from the high jump.

Gerald Bastow was awakened by the torpedo and proceeded to dress, but when the lights went, decided he had better get out. He was half-dressed and had one sock half-on.

Even as Gerald Bastow and Bob Butt reached the deck, the *Caribou* sank beneath them. Bastow thought, *This is it!*

He had often heard about the terrific suction of a sinking ship, but he was a good swimmer, used to the salt water, and as he was being pulled under he began to swim strongly.

William Lundrigan (left) and Thomas Fleming.

Gerald kept swimming but had the terrible feeling he wasn't making any headway. Above him the water seemed flooded with light, but he felt he wasn't reaching it at all, then suddenly he was making headway. He broke the surface. Later, he figured he had been under about half a minute.

There were rafts in the vicinity, but the first one was too overloaded and must have been damaged, because she overturned and broke up. They all made for the remaining life rafts and climbed aboard.

Charles Moores was thrown from his berth, but his companion wasn't even awakened. He shook him awake and they dressed quickly, but before they had a chance to adjust their lifebelts properly, the ship was plunged into darkness.

The main deck was already awash when they reached topside, and the stern of the *Caribou* was rising as she slid beneath the seas. Charles made his way to the quarterdeck, and here men and women were shouting and screaming, trying to get rafts into the sea. One woman, wearing a lifebelt, hung onto the railing, crying with fear, and Charles forced her to release her grip and made her jump into the sea. Then, something hit him in the back and flung him overboard.

He came to, fighting his way to the surface of the sea minus his lifebelt, and made for a piece of wreckage.

Thomas Fleming, the purser, was thrown from his bunk, and in a second he was awake and alert. "We've got the works, Bill," he said to his assistant.

On deck, they saw Captain Tavenor struggling into his coat, and Tom paused to help him. Then he saw the captain go up to the bridge, with Bill Hogan following.

He made for a life raft to release it, but its mechanism was stuck, and even as they worked at it the *Caribou* slid beneath the waves, carrying Tom Fleming with her.

Tom was horribly conscious of the fact that he was being pulled down by the *Caribou*, but he was a strong swimmer and fought against it. In his mind there was a grim determination to reach the surface, and finally, with his lungs near bursting point, he did.

The survivors of the sinking of the SS *Caribou* on the deck of the Royal Canadian Navy minesweeper *Grandmere*, on her way to North Sydney, Nova Scotia.

In the sea, people were fighting to live, while others gave up the struggle and died. Two lifeboats had gotten away from the *Caribou*, but one had sunk because the plugs had been taken out, and the other was in peril of sinking until a crew member hurriedly plugged the four holes in her.

Bob Newman, a businessman of Petites who had boarded the *Caribou* at the last minute, was unable to swim a stroke, but miraculously threshed his way from the sinking *Caribou* to the wreckage.

Gerald Bastow and his friend Bob Butt survived the *Caribou* sinking, but his school friend, Edgar Martin, was among the 137 who became victims of the disaster, which left twenty-one widows and fifty-one orphans in Port aux Basques and Channel.

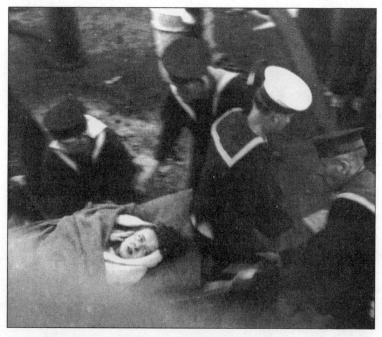

Anxiety shows on the face of this survivor of the sinking of the SS *Caribou* as she and others are carried ashore from the rescue ship *Grandmere* at North Sydney, Nova Scotia.

Here, the only baby to survive the sinking of the SS *Caribou* is held by one of the crewmen aboard the RCN minesweeper *Grandmere*, en route to North Sydney with the survivors.

Death March

THE STORY OF A SEALING DISASTER

TUESDAY, MARCH 31, 1914

At dawning, the day showed great promise as the sun eased up over the glittering white rim of the icefields. It was beautiful and still, and the morning glowed and brightened as the red-gold ball of fire cleared the rim and climbed slowly into a cloudless sky.

In the middle of the lonely expanse of the icefields, half a dozen ships were coming to life, getting up steam to force their way through the heavy, Arctic ice.

Some forty miles to the west lay the great rock-bound island of Newfoundland, and it was from this windswept sentinel of the western world these ships had come, manned by hardy Newfoundlanders, who were eager to be off on the hunt for seals. For this was the time of the seal hunters, who sailed north every spring to meet the heavy Arctic ice and to garner the rich harvest of the Arctic seals as their ancestors had done before them, and their ancestors before that.

The day broadened, and there was much activity as the men swarmed over the ships' sides to begin panning for seals, for seal fat meant money. All ships were only a few miles apart and doing fairly well.

With the exception of one.

The SS *Newfoundland*, her wooden decks steaming in the heat of the early morning sun, was jammed solidly in the ice. Great pans of the heavy ice had rafted around her hull, and she could move neither forward nor backward. She hadn't panned or taken on board a single seal since the previous Saturday.

For three days the crew had chafed at the enforced idleness, for they weren't earning until they were "in the seals." Furthermore, the *Newfoundland* was the only ship in the fleet with no wireless—she was completely out of contact with the rest of the world.

However, on this bright and beautiful morning, no wireless was needed to tell them about the other ships' progress. The young captain, Westbury Kean, and the second hand, George Tuff, stood in the barrel gazing toward the SS *Stephano* a few miles distant. With the powerful telescope, the captain could see the crew of the other ships, at work on the ice, panning seals.

"It's hard to see the other ships in the seals, and us not able to reach them," he said to George Tuff.

George Tuff, who was a reliable, experienced sealer, said eagerly, "We can walk to them easily, Captain. 'Tis only a few miles."

It was what the captain wanted to hear, for although most sealers travel for miles on the ice when they're already "in the seals," a captain would not order his men on the ice until they were reasonably close.

"You're a good man, George." Once again he scanned the ice with his telescope while he made up his mind, then he turned to the second hand. "Get the men together, and tell them to get ready to hit the ice."

"Yes sir!"

"Head for the *Stephano*; Father will put you on to some seals. Meantime, I'll go check the glass."

Westbury Kean's father was Captain Abram Kean of the *Stephano*, a hardy experienced old sailor who'd spent many seasons at the seal hunt. He could be relied upon to direct them to a good patch of seals.

The SS *Newfoundland* in 1914. Seventy-eight of her ill-clad sealers died after spending two days and nights on the ice, exposed to wind, frost, and snow.

The glass was normal, but the sky had clouded over at 7:00 A.M. when about 150 men swarmed over the *Newfoundland*'s side. "If weather comes on, you can reckon on the *Stephano*," Captain Kean shouted to George.

Unfortunately, in the bustle and confusion of men hitting the ice, George Tuff did not hear his captain's order.

The crew divided into four watches and picked their way over the difficult, treacherous ice. It was reckoned the *Stephano* was about four or five miles away, but it was soon apparent that she was much farther than she had appeared to be. The men did not complain. They were anxious to get into the seals.

By mid-morning the sky had grown dark and heavy. The young captain followed his men's progress through the telescope, and noticed at ten o'clock that some of the men had stopped.

Ah, he thought. *They're in the seals.*

He was puzzled when he saw they weren't scattering as they should have been, but some were walking steadily back to his ship. The rest of the crew continued their trek to the *Stephano*, and he followed their progress through the telescope.

Heavy, snow-laden clouds gathered quickly, and large, lazy snowflakes began to fall, and somewhat anxiously now, he kept his eyes on the small black dots that were his men.

It was around noon when they gathered around the *Stephano*, and the young captain gave a sigh of relief, rubbed his eyes, and went to greet the first of the watch who were returning to the ship.

"There warn't a seal in sight, sir. Not much use in going on," one sealer growled.

"I don't like the looks of that sky, sir. I seen the sun hounds, and that's not a good sign," another muttered.

Then the men shifted uneasily. They weren't too happy about returning to the ship empty-handed, but it was a well-known fact that "sun hounds" were the forerunner of bad weather.

The young captain found it difficult to conceal his disappointment. "All right, men, you'd better get some dinner," he said, and immediately hurried to consult the barometer. To his immense relief, it was steady.

This bit of snow meant nothing. It was too soft, too mild. Besides, if it got too dirty, his other men were already aboard the *Stephano* and were quite safe.

The *Newfoundland*'s crew were welcomed aboard the *Stephano*. Despite the long, heavy walk they were in good spirits and among themselves decided they had come not four or five miles as they had first supposed, but a good seven or eight miles. Their own ship, concealed by high, rafted ice, could not be seen by the naked eye, even if it hadn't been snowing.

They went below deck for a "mug-up," and George Tuff sought out Captain Abram Kean for information as to the whereabouts of seals.

"There's a patch of seals a mile or so to the sou'west," the old skipper told him.

It was snowing thickly and the wind had sprung up. By the time the men had finished eating, Captain Kean and George Tuff agreed that, though it was "dirty," it was too mild to amount to anything. The glass was steady. There was nothing to fear.

"Over the side, men," Captain Kean roared. "The seals are yonder to the sou'west." A few men demurred as they peered through the thickly falling snow, and a New Perlican man said flatly that if someone would stay with him, he'd not get on the ice. His buddies rallied around him and good-naturedly persuaded him over the rail. He went reluctantly.

"Step lively, now, I've got men of my own to pick up," the captain shouted. "The *Newfoundland*'s quite near, so you'll be all right."

The optical illusion that led George Tuff to believe the *Stephano* was only four or five miles from his own ship also led the old skipper to believe the *Newfoundland* was quite near. It appears no one corrected him. Abram Kean made sure all the men were safe on the ice, then he ordered the *Stephano* north. He was soon out of sight.

The soft, wet snow drove against them, and it was difficult for the men to see where they were going. They had divided into three watches (about forty men in each) but stuck closely together as a precautionary measure. About half a mile from where the *Stephano* had left them, they struck a small patch of scattered seals. These they killed, and in about twenty minutes were all together again.

The wind was increasing in force, and the snow was thickening so a man couldn't see the length of himself. George Tuff gathered the men around him. "The best thing to do is return to the ship."

There was a chorus of agreement.

"We'll all keep together so none of us will get lost."

To take a bearing was impossible, so they started out in the direction they thought the *Newfoundland* lay. The wind whistled across the ice and struck at them, and snow clung to their eyebrows and eyelashes, blinding them.

Then they were hurrying as best they could over the rough ice, for it was evident this was turning into a storm—a mild one, but a storm nevertheless. But the hours passed and still there was no sign of their ship.

At last, bone-tired and weary, they stopped and decided the three watches should separate, in the hope that one would reach a ship—any ship—and send out word of their plight.

So, with the wind howling around their ears and the snow shutting out the world, the three watches separated and melted into the whirling whiteness.

The first man to lag and complain of weariness was a middle-aged sealer who wore glasses. He couldn't see without them—nor with them—because of the snow. He fell behind, groping blindly with his gaff.

But George Tuff, the second hand, bringing up the rear to sight stragglers, spotted him. He took the man firmly by the arm and guided his faltering footsteps as he uttered words of encouragement.

They trudged on and on, leaning more heavily on their gaffs, but there was only the snow and the wind, and the rough ice beneath their feet, and for most it meant wet feet and legs as they stumbled from ice pan to ice pan.

The wind blew stronger, and the spirits of these courageous men began to fall. It was no longer a mere

The *Newfoundland*. Inset is Captain Westbury Kean, son of Captain Abram Kean.

Sealers, warmly dressed and equipped with gaffs and poles, await the order from the skipper before they swarm over the ship's side to harvest a patch of seals on the ice.

storm but a raging blizzard, and they were weary, hungry, and lost!

Nor did it help matters any when, just before dark, their other two watches, wandering blindly on the ice, joined them. It meant that no one had reached a ship.

They crowded close for a consultation. One hundred and twenty-eight men, not scared or unduly worried yet, but anxious, formed a questioning circle around the second hand.

"Well, men," he said, "this looks as good a night as any to stay on the ice."

The men shifted uneasily and murmured amongst themselves, but there was no outcry, no protest. The three watches separated again, this time to find a safe, large ice pan on which to spend the night.

The wind, though violent, was still blowing from the southwest and remained quite mild, but to protect themselves from the violence of it the men went to work with their gaffs, jabbing and breaking the tall pinnacles of ice that had formed on the pans, picking up the pieces and building themselves a protective wall.

Then they dug into their meagre rations of hardtack, and the mixture of oatmeal, raisins, and sugar they carried in a small sack, and shared it around. Those whose feet had gotten wet stamped and danced jigs to warm themselves while the others cheered them on

This wasn't too bad, they agreed—uncomfortable, but the weather was mild. Soon it would stop snowing, and they would spot the lights of a ship and make for it.

The crew of the *Bellaventure* collect the bodies of sealers from the *Newfoundland*.

But they were wrong. Quite wrong.

The day that had begun so beautifully with a golden sunrise was not to pass into oblivion without taking a few souls with it. About nine o'clock that night, without a lull or a warning, the gale winds suddenly chopped around the northeast. The temperature dropped rapidly, and soft, wet snow became icy pellets that bit savagely into the human flesh.

Still jammed tightly, the *Newfoundland* lay where she had been for days, but there was no anxiety on board. Captain Westbury Kean was confident his men were safe and sound on board his father's ship, the *Stephano*.

Aboard the *Stephano*, Captain Abram Kean was equally confident the *Newfoundland*'s men were aboard their own ship. The SS *Florizel*, another sealing ship about five miles distant, had wired earlier that she had picked up Captain Abram Kean's crew, and he returned immediately to the position where he'd dropped George Tuff and his men, and though there was no sign of them, he kept his whistle blowing at intervals...just in case. George Tuff was a good, level-headed man and no doubt had his men on board hours ago.

Nonetheless, he wished the *Newfoundland* had a wireless. He could contact them and know for sure.

Meanwhile, on the ice the three separate watches of some forty-odd souls in each huddled together for warmth, some singing to keep up their spirits, others dancing and skylarking. But there were some who were weary to the bone and unable to dance or sing. The bitter cold seeped into their bodies, into the very marrow of their bones, as the temperature dropped rapidly to zero.

The grim reaper was not too far away.

The bitter wind blew with hurricane force. It howled through the rigging of the ships, and snow hissed through the air to hit the decks like tiny grains of sand driven by the force of the wind.

On the ice, a small fire flickered. A few far-sighted hunters had dragged along some seals they had killed earlier. They had broken their gaffs and somehow started a fire. Now, over the red flames they roasted the hearts and shared them around, then they skinned the seals and put the dripping, oily pelts on the fire.

Despite the wall of ice they had built, and despite the fire, the intense cold, helped by the wind, bit deeply into their bones. Some of the older men, though used to hardships, were physically exhausted after hours of wandering on the rough ice, and beyond the fire there were some who could not move or push themselves toward the life-giving heat, nor did they have the inclination. It was much easier to fall asleep.

The wiser ones kept moving among the inert figures and with punches and shouts forced them to move; dragged them to the fire; shook them; made them walk.

But the night was long. The bitter wind numbed their bodies. Snow froze onto their eyebrows and lashes. Bearded men had their faces encrusted with ice.

When some of these men became too weak to remove the ice from their faces and eyes, young Jesse Collins of the Labrador gallantly bit it off for them. His own lips became frostbitten while doing so, but throughout the night his strong teeth bit away the ice that kept forming over the older ones' eyes.

Young Albert Crewe of Elliston kept an anxious eye on his father, Reuben. If his dad showed the inclination to fall asleep, the young man worked frantically to keep him awake...and alive.

Throughout the harsh, bitter night, there was great courage on three pans of ice. Sometime midway through the snow thinned and finally stopped, but they were unaware of it because the wind still blew at hurricane strength and the ground drift was blinding.

The younger, more energetic men kept up the morale of the oldsters. They danced and poked and boxed as if they were having a wonderful time of it. They coaxed and wheedled and roughhoused those who lay on the ice to die, but despite their best efforts the grey, icy dawn revealed a few still bodies.

The shock of seeing their comrades curled up in death on the ice had a disheartening effect on the exhausted men, but it also served as a grim reminder of what happened to those who did not keep on the move.

As the day lightened, their spirits lifted. They had spent a very bad night on the ice, and a great many of them were suffering from frostbite, but soon...a few hours maybe...their troubles would be over, they would be safe and sound on their ship and snug in their berths.

They were hungry, too.

Man, but they were hungry!

The few remaining cakes of hardtack were scrupulously shared. Then the three watches came together, the strong encouraging the weak.

The ground drift made it difficult for them to see far, and it was decided they should strike toward the southeast, with an admonition from George Tuff to stick closely together.

It was still bitterly cold, and the men, already numb beyond feeling, decided they should remove the heavy outer clothing from the dead.

There were some who murmured against this, and one of these was James Donovan of Petty Harbour, who had somehow lost his cap in the blizzard.

"It's not right," he growled.

"What difference does it make? They won't know the difference," his younger brother Stephen argued. "Here, take this cap."

But no amount of persuasion, even by young Stephen, could make him take a cap from any of the dead men.

Despite the few protests, it was agreed that it was the sensible thing to do. Then, having shared the clothing, the seal hunters started the march across the ice.

Up in the barrel of the *Newfoundland*, Captain Westbury Kean kept his spyglass trained on the *Stephano*. There were men on the ice in the immediate vicinity of the ship, but the ground drift was so bad he caught only occasional glimpses of them, and he wondered if it was his men working the seals.

The ice had loosened a bit during the storm, and he wasn't jammed anymore. He decided to get up steam, make his way toward the *Stephano*, and take his own men on board.

He gave the order, and soon the *Newfoundland* was butting her way slowly through the heavy ice. All hands on board were confident their comrades were panning seals and were waiting to be picked up.

There was no let-up in the wind.

It howled across the ice, swirling the fine snow before it, helping the frost to bite more deeply into their flesh, and in the white, glittering world of ice, eyes became glazed and unseeing.

Groping their way from pan to pan, the blind ones relied on their companions to help them along, for they were almost as helpless as babies, but even the hardiest of them were reeling from cold and exhaustion now.

They strung along, stumbling, falling, feeling their way with their gaffs, weaving like drunks on the heaving ice. Many fell to their knees in slush as they moved from pan to pan and would have died there, but the man behind would step up and drag him to his feet, and they moved automatically on and on,

Time passed. Each minute was an hour, each hour an eternity, and still there was nothing but ice and snow and the bitter, bitter cold.

By midday they began to drop, and most of them were dead before they hit the ice.

Then Cecil Miller of Newtown raised a frostbitten hand over his frostbitten face and squinted through the swirling snow. It suddenly registered on his befuddled and benumbed brain that for some time he had been seeing something. Then he gave a croak.

"A steamer, boys, a steamer. We're saved!"

The word passed slowly down the wavering line, and dull eyes brightened as hope sparked life into the benumbed bodies and brains of the men. One of the hardiest ran to a pinnacle of ice, climbed and waved a sealing flag he carried.

Eyes that could see and eyes that could not see strained eagerly through the drift for that longed-for sight, and sure enough, there she was, not more than a mile or so away, a steamer slowing butting her way through the ice...the most beautiful sight in the world.

The dying and the near dead gained new strength in the knowledge that help was so near, and they staggered or crawled over the ice, encouraged by the croaking cheers from the stronger ones.

Then...it became apparent that the steamer hadn't seen them. She was passing them by.

The cheers became frantic shouts, and strong men wept as she faded from sight. Some just stared, their faces passive and blank as if they did not comprehend the whole thing at all, or care. Others keeled over and died.

It was slow going for the *Newfoundland*. She had butted her way to within a mile or so of the *Stephano*, but the rafting ice once more made it impossible for her to move any closer, nor could the captain put his men on the ice. It was too dangerous.

There was nothing to do but wait it out. The ice had to loosen its grip before he could get his men transferred back to his own ship.

It was hard to accept that help had been so near, only to pass them by. The men stared dully in the direction she'd disappeared, then quietly, resignedly, they plodded on.

Their bodies no longer felt the bitter cold. They lifted one foot, then the other, and as the hours passed, men began to drop like ninepins. Those bringing up the rear removed the heavy outer garments from the dead and distributed them among themselves.

Albert and Reuben Crewe staggered along together. When the older man showed signs of failing, his son rallied long enough to croak words of encouragement, and if the son fell to the ice from sheer exhaustion, the old man exerted his failing strength to make his son get up and to keep going. Somehow...somehow, they did keep going.

James Donovan, bare-headed and frostbitten, plodded on, his main concern being young Stephen, who kept falling and wanting to rest. James's hair was white with snow and frost, but he doggedly passed every dead sealer without taking a cap, despite young Stephen's pleas.

The wind and the frost whistled and crackled around them, and Stephen fell more often, his eyes glazed, his mind wandering. Suddenly, without a sound, he pitched forward and fell like a log...dead before he hit the ice.

James knelt clumsily beside his brother, his mind unable to grasp that young Stephen was dead. For a long time he remained there as the other sealers staggered by in twos and threes, and at last he decided he, too, had better move on if he didn't want to drop dead. But before rising, he tenderly removed the cap from Stephen's head and placed it on his own.

Under the circumstances, Stephen would have wanted him to have it.

And so the death march continued.

The bitter hours dragged slowly. The human beings staggering through the drifting snow were like automatons. Their movements were mechanical, their faces slack, and their eyes blank. The only indication they had that their minds were still functioning was when they emitted an occasional croak of encouragement to their dying comrades.

Only years of experience led most of them safely from ice pan to ice pan. But now, after more then twenty-four hours' exposure to the bitter, freezing elements, men's minds began to snap.

One stopped and straightened, his eyes held a strange, faraway look. "I'm going to the fo'c'sle," he said clearly and, walking to the edge of the pan, stepped deliberately into the sea. Another man did the same, only he thought he was entering his own home.

On they plodded, more like walking zombies than flesh-and-blood human beings. Now when the men dropped, the survivors could not encourage them back to their feet; they merely stepped over or around them. Others, in raving delirium, stepped into the sea, thinking they were going to their beds, or to dinner.

Miraculously, a few of the survivors' minds were functioning enough to kill two or three seals they spotted before dark, and, mindful of the night before, they secured their kill with ropes and towed them along.

George Tuff, haggard and exhausted but still in full command of his faculties, halted the wavering line at dusk. "We'll camp on this ice pan, men."

Left: Captain Abram Kean, skipper of the *Stephano*.
Right: George Tuff, second hand on the *Newfoundland*.

Wordlessly they gathered around, the strong encouraging the weak. One man squatted on the ice beside the frozen carcass of the seals and with frozen fingers gripped a knife, and somehow skinned a seal.

Someone found matches that weren't soaked through and, after much difficulty, got a fire started. They roasted the seal hearts and the seal meat and shared it around, but there were men who died in the very act of eating, their hearts worn out from sheer exhaustion.

Again they burned the pelts and their gaffs and did their best to keep alive. The father and son, Albert and Reuben Crewe, had made the heartbreaking journey so far, but now the older man was ready to give up the fight. The son, gaunt and hollow-eyed, put his arms around his father and held him close. "Hang on, Father," he coaxed. "Hang on just another little while."

But even as he spoke, his brave, anxious heart stopped beating, and still holding his father in his arms, he toppled over. Neither moved again.

Sometime during the night the wind dropped, but the cold grew more intense, and men, claiming they were going to their bunks, laid themselves on the ice and died. More wandered away and died alone. Several lost their reason completely and beat themselves until the blood flowed freely.

The ice beneath them, packed loosely now because of the storm, heaved dangerously, but the men seemed unaware of it. They gazed vacantly into space, living in a strange, silent world of their own, no longer affected by the bitter dark night surrounding them.

They raved deliriously about their homes and families, speaking lovingly or scoldingly to imaginary wives or children before they died. They died sitting, standing, and praying on their knees...and there were some who died in the act of singing to keep up their morale.

At long last, it was daybreak, and with daybreak came new hope, for with no ground drift to plague them they discovered two ships on the horizon.

George Tuff spoke up. "It's every man for himself. I'm going to make for the *Newfoundland*, if anybody wants to come with me, but the quicker we get to the boat the better off we'll be. Only eight others had the reserve energy to fall in with George Tuff. The remainder were too exhausted to make it on their own and decided to stay where they were until help arrived.

Six miles away, the barrelman of the SS *Bellaventure* trained his spyglass on a group of men in the middle of the icefield, thinking they were "in the seals." His eyes sharpened as he watched, then he was down out of the barrel and running for the captain.

"Men in trouble, sir. There's a bunch of 'em out there, and they're wobbling all over the place."

The captain took one hurried look through the spyglass, then gave orders for his crew to take to the ice with food, blankets, and stimulants. Over six miles of rough ice they hurried to their fellow men, but even as they neared victims at long last, not even the promise of food, warmth, and safety could keep some alive.

Pat Hearn, a nineteen-year-old youth whose bright, cheerful disposition had done much to keep up the

In St. John's, thousands of relatives, friends, and curious onlookers await the arrival of bodies and survivors of the SS *Newfoundland* disaster of 1914.

morale of others, spotted the rescuers, although he was suffering slightly from snow blindness, and at that crucial moment the strain of two day and two nights on the ice told on the lad. The light of reason left his eyes as he wheeled and ran blindly from his comrades and rescuers too.

At the same time, Captain Westbury Kean was in the barrel of his ship, which was still securely jammed. His spyglass swept the ice, looking for his men. He was more than anxious to have them back on board his own ship after forty-eight hours.

As he watched their progress he got the shock of his life, for he could see plainly that the men were staggering and weaving about the ice like drunks. It struck him with the force of a blow that his men had been on the ice since Tuesday.

White and shaken, he left the barrel and got to the deck, where he gathered the rest of his crew and gave them the dreaded news. "Get food and stimulants, and get them fast," he ordered and, being in a state of near collapse with shock himself, was assisted to his cabin.

"If only we'd had a wireless," he growled. "This wouldn't have happened."

If.

Out in the icefields, the crew of the *Bellaventure* met and mingled with the survivors. One man died while they were in the act of forcing the burning, life-giving stimulant down his throat. Another stumbled toward them with a glad cry and fell to his knees. He was dead when they picked him up.

There were thirty-five sealers to be taken back to the *Bellaventure*, and of these thirty-five only a handful

The frozen corpses tell the gruesome tale. Seventy-seven bodies of sealers from the SS *Newfoundland* are seen here stacked on the deck of the SS *Bellaventure*, the ship which brought the remains to St. John's.

Coffins await the unlucky victims of the SS *Newfoundland* disaster.

could stagger along on their own. The remainder were completely helpless.

Meanwhile, young Pat Hearn stumbled around in the great white wilderness all by himself, blind to the glare and glitter of the ice and quite out of his mind.

From ship to ship the news of the disaster was flashed, from the *Bellaventure* to the *Stephano*, and the *Florizel*. Other ships nearby picked up the messages, too. Only the *Newfoundland* was out of contact, and she was still helpless in the grip of the Arctic ice.

The crews of all the ships hit the ice in search of possible survivors and to pick up the dead. It was easy to follow the corpse-strewn trail that weaved across the ice, and the *Bellaventure*'s crew gathered fifty dead bodies that first day.

It was a gruesome, heart-rending task, for the frozen bodies were in all sorts of positions. Some were kneeling in an attitude of prayer, some were curled up as if sleeping in their own beds, others who had fallen while dancing or singing held their arms and legs in frozen supplication.

A raving, delirious young man picked up by the *Stephano*'s crew was identified as young Pat Hearn. With the resilience of youth, he recovered speedily.

For days the hunt was forgotten as the crews searched the icefields for the dead. The final count was seventy-seven dead and forty-seven survivors. (One of these survivors died in hospital, bringing the death toll to seventy-eight). Sixty-nine bodies were found; the other eight were those who had deliberately walked into the sea.

They were never found.

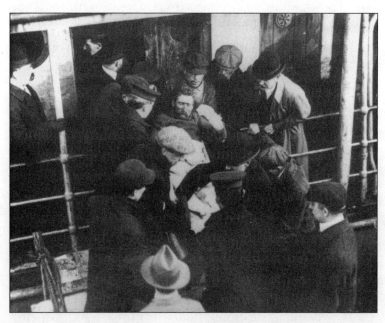

Lucky to be alive. A survivor is taken off the ship.

In the investigation that followed, feelings ran high as the court listened to the stories of all the survivors in detail. Letters to the papers angrily denounced old Captain Abram Kean for ordering the sealers on the ice in bad weather. Others blamed Captain Westbury Kean. However, in the final analysis the court ruled that no one person was to blame.

It was a sad, unfortunate incident caused by a freak storm. The barometer had given no indication of a storm, and since captains had to rely on their barometers for weather, they could not honestly, or fairly, be blamed. Both were exonerated.

And so ended one of the worst sealing disasters in the history of Newfoundland.

Survived Because of Love

CECIL MOULAND'S STORY

In times of great disaster, when death seems inevitable, there are many things that give man the will to stick it out just a little while longer.

On March 31, 1914, when over 150 men of the SS *Newfoundland* were caught in a raging blizzard on the icefields off the northeast coast of Newfoundland during the annual seal hunt, seventy-eight men would die and the survivors would have been exposed to the vicious elements in zero-degree weather.

Cecil Mouland of Doting Cove, Bonavista Bay, a cheerful man with a sunny disposition, was not twenty years old when he went to the icefields that year on the *Newfoundland*, and he survived because he was in love. Said Cecil, "I was courting a girl at that time, and I wondered who was going to have her if I died out on the ice. I made up my mind nobody else was going to get her."

It was as simple as that.

Today, October 27, 1964, he still has that girl, and they are celebrating their forty-ninth wedding anniversary.

Going back to the *Newfoundland* disaster, Cecil Mouland recalls that they left the *Newfoundland* around 7:00 A.M. and made it to the *Stephano* around noon. It was snowing a little and they got aboard and had a mug-up, but some of them hadn't finished their mug-up before they were ordered over the side.

Young Cecil Mouland.

"We left everything up to the second hand, George Tuff," said Cecil. "But when Captain Kean told us we had to walk back to our own ship in such weather, we began to murmur like the children of Israel in the wilderness. We went for George like they went for Moses.

"That night we were waist-deep in snow. It was a real blizzard, and we began to get uneasy although it was snowing first, then raining and not too bad, but halfway through the night the wind chopped around and it began to freeze. It was a bad night after that."

In Cecil's crowd, six men died that night. Two of the men fell in the water but were pulled out. However, the wet sealers lay on the ice, and that is where they died.

They selected Jesse Collins as their boss, and he decided they should go through the motions of fishing in order to keep warm. First they went jigging, and he'd say, "There's not much on the jigger today, b'ys."

They all agreed and Mr. Collins would say, "We'll go with hook and line." They would bait their imaginary hooks with imaginary caplin and throw out another line, pulling in and in until they got warm.

When that was finished, Jesse Collins would say, "All right b'ys, we'll go on parade now," and they would line up single file and march around and around, hitting one another on the shoulder. Then they would stop and huddle together, and everyone would try to get in the middle, boring in through the crowd. "Next thing, you'd be on the outside," said Cecil Mouland.

Cecil never stopped or sat down. He watched all the fellows as they gave up. All would say, "I'm awful tired and sleepy. I think I'll sit down for five minutes and take a little rest."

They sat down and never got up.

Cecil saw his own cousin, Ralph Mouland, lay down to die, and he said to him, "You going to die, Ralph?"

Ralph replied, "Yes, I can't stick it out any longer."

Said Cecil, "Well, I wouldn't die if I were you. I wouldn't give it to them to say back home that you died on this old ice." He then got Ralph to his feet, punched him and pushed him around, rousing him thoroughly. "He came through," said Cecil, "and died only a few years ago."

After the sealing disaster, Cecil Mouland moved to Brooklyn, New York, where he eventually became an American citizen. At the outbreak of World War II, the U.S. government asked for carpenters to volunteer to go around the world to build army, navy, and air force bases. Naturally, Cecil volunteered for Newfoundland!

But he was working one day at Fort Pepperell when he was stricken with pneumonia, from which he suffered a relapse. After he had recuperated from that he was run over by a car on Prince of Wales Street, right opposite Buckmaster's Field gate, was dragged about a hundred feet, and suffered: over a dozen broken ribs, each broken in three places; a broken collar bone; and cuts and bruises. He was in hospital on a fracture board for six weeks.

Cecil returned to the United States after the war, but when he retired at the age of sixty-five, Cecil and his wife, Jessie, came back to Newfoundland to live and bought a home in Hare Bay, Bonavista bay. He has been here for six years and has applied to become a Canadian citizen.

This year, the fiftieth anniversary of the *Newfoundland* sealing disaster, Cecil Mouland was trying to get together all the thirteen survivors for a reunion, but the men were too scattered.

Jessie and Cecil Mouland. As a young man, the thought of losing his sweetheart Jessie to another man motivated Cecil Mouland to do all in his power to survive his ordeal on the ice.

Cecil attained his seventy-first birthday September 27 and still retains his sunny disposition. Said Mrs. Mouland, "I don't think there's anyone else like him. He's a very nice man. I don't know what I'd do without him."

Mr. Mouland is a Salvation Army man, and at one period was an usher for Billy Graham for four months.

Death March

WESLEY COLLINS'S STORY

If ever a man seemed destined to die at sea, Wesley Collins appeared to be one of that breed, for the ever-hungry seas tried to claim him not once, but three times.

Wesley Collins is sixty-nine years of age (1964) and is one of the few remaining survivors of the SS *Newfoundland* disaster fifty years ago, but he is young and vigorous despite his years.

Mr. Collins, recalling the beginning of those fateful two days, says that it was snowing a bit when the sealers boarded the *Stephano* after their four-hour trek over the ice from his own ship the *Newfoundland*, but it was "snowing good" after they'd had a mug-up and were ordered on the ice by Captain Abram Kean, through the master watches.

Says Wesley, who was nineteen years of age at that time, "When we got to the seals, it was too stormy to stop. We started to go for our ship and we walked and walked until it got dark."

When George Tuff, the second hand, told them they would have to spend the night on the ice, they didn't mind too much because they were confident that they'd be picked up in the morning.

It was, he said, rough, snowing, and blowing, and a scattered man died that night. The wind had veered and it got cold, but it really got bitterly cold Wednesday night when the snow started to drift.

"The first night we sang, danced, and pretended we were jigging for squid, working our hands, doing any kind of exercise to keep us busy," said Wesley. "But we couldn't keep that up for long because we were hungry and weak."

On Wednesday, as they marched over the ice, they'd see a hole in the distance and think it was a ship. "We were wet, our clothes were frozen, and after so many hours of constant exposure we couldn't even think," said Mr. Collins. "We went on and on automatically."

Wesley's right leg was frozen. He knew this because it was stiff and dead, but he kept walking like a robot and kept moving around to keep himself alive during that bitter second night on the ice. On the third morning, men were dropping like flies, but it did not affect Wesley any more. Nobody had the strength to encourage anybody else. It was every man for himself, and the great majority barely had enough life in them to keep moving on their own.

Two Port Rexton men from the *Bellaventure* helped him over the ice to the safety of the ship after they were found about 11:00 A.M. Thursday, but Wesley didn't have to be carried.

Mr. Collins feels that Captain Westbury Kean was not to blame for the disaster. "He was a good man, and he was not to blame for what happened."

Wesley Collins never actively participated in the seal fishery again because he lost that frozen right leg and all the toes on his left leg, but he went to the ice with Captain Westbury Kean for four seasons, working aboard ship.

Despite the loss of his leg, Wesley Collins kept going to sea. One of his bunkmates on the *Newfoundland*, another young sealer by the name of Hedley Payne, had survived the dreadful ordeal without the loss of any limbs or even frostbite. In 1918, Payne was master of the sailing vessel *A.J. Stirling*, which was scheduled to sail across the ocean with a load of fish for Naples.

Wesley went along as a member of the crew, and after twenty-eight days they arrived at their destination. After discharging their freight the vessel sailed for home, but they ran into a gale of wind along the coast of Sardinia that blew away all their canvas and drove her up on shore, and the crew had to abandon her. They got into their dories and rowed to an island off the African coast. A French destroyer took them off the island and landed them in Bizerta, and from there to Marseilles, France, where they signed on a Hudson Bay Co. ship to New York. They arrived home in Newfoundland April 4, 1919.

Wesley's last adventure on the seas took place the following month when he joined with Captain John Barbour of Newtown, Bonavista Bay, and his two sons, Daniel and Douglas, to bring a schooner from Canada to Newfoundland.

Captain Barbour was purchasing a fishing schooner in a community on Lake Bras d'Or, but having arrived there and given the schooner a going-over decided she wasn't worth buying. They had to hire a boat then to take them back to Mulgrave, since the ferry had not come to the community that morning.

Captain Barbour hired a lobster boat and its owner, Colin Digton, to take them to the ferry terminal, but the little boat, loaded with luggage and five men, was suddenly caught in a crosswind and capsized.

Wesley, unable to swim, went down, but came up immediately beside the boat, which was filled to the gunwales with water, and the owner, standing up to his waist in water. Of Captain Barbour and his two sons there was no sign.

Wesley Collins grabbed the gunwale of the boat and hung on as it drifted with the wind and tide. Colin Digton was helpless to assist him. He dared not move to try and pull Wesley aboard, for if the water in the boat shifted she would just roll under, taking them both.

Wesley Collins says he felt worse during this predicament than he had during the *Newfoundland* disaster. Since he was unable to swim, he didn't know but that next minute would be his last. Every time a lop came over his head, he didn't know if it might take the boat and all.

"I had to hold on," he said, "and blow the water out of my mouth like a whale."

The boat drifted ashore two hours later at Laskey Point, and the lightkeeper spotted them and helped them to safety.

Captain John Barbour's body was found later, but the bodies of his two sons were never found. Wesley came home with the body of Captain John, accompanied it to Newtown, Bonavista Bay, then came back to St. John's.

"I went to sea once more on the *Nancy Lee* to Sydney for a load of coal, then I gave it up."

Having lost eighty-one shipmates at sea was enough to turn any man from the sea.

The FLORIZEL Disaster

At 4:50 A.M. on a stormy winter's dawn, the Red Cross Liner SS *Florizel* steamed full speed ahead in angry seas, to her doom. With a passenger list of seventy-eight and a crew of sixty the ship moved steadily through the darkness, rolling and pitching in the turbulent, shallow waters, and not until she struck and was impaled upon the rocks was her captain and crew aware that they had run the proud ship right on the shore. They had even seen the warning white of breakers ahead but had mistakenly assumed it to be a slob of ice and, despite the alarming pitch and roll of the ship, continued full speed ahead.

The *Florizel* had left the port of St. John's at 8:00 P.M. on Saturday, February 23, 1918, for Halifax and New York. About an hour or so later, a southeast gale and snowstorm came on and continued until midnight, when the wind chopped around to east-northeast, blowing with equal violence.

On the *Florizel*, Captain William Martin was unworried. He had a sound ship, his equipment was good, and although it was a stormy night, the *Florizel* was, in his opinion, capable of holding her own.

Slob ice prevented the use of the log, which was the only accurate means of judging the speed of the ship.

Although she was supposed to be making ten to twelve knots throughout the night and early hours of Sunday, Captain Martin, allowing for wind, sea, and ice, allotted her only six knots as a measure of precaution, so that when he ordered her course changed to west-by-south he was sure he was well and safely out in the Atlantic and beyond Cape Race and headed for Halifax. He was doubly confident since they had been steaming for nine hours on a six-hour run.

Captain Martin.

One uneasy passenger who prowled restlessly around the ship that night was Captain Joe Kean, bound for Halifax to pick up a ship. He visited the captain on the bridge around 4:00 A.M. and was apparently reassured by the captain's confidence. But Captain Martin was dangerously close to land, and when he ordered the change in course, the bow of the *Florizel* pointed straight at the land, and within ten minutes she was hard and fast on Horn Head Point just off from Cappahayden on the Southern Shore.

She struck amidships, listed to the starboard and immediately began to settle astern as the violent seas crashed in over her. Although she struck with terrific force, some passengers felt the crash more than others, and some passengers even had time to dress before leaving their staterooms. Others were almost immediately forced from their rooms by the rushing seas.

Amazingly enough there seemed to be no great panic. Alex Ledingham, an engineer and first-class passenger, helped some steerage passengers into lifebelts when they came looking for them, then they all made their way to the stairway leading up to the deck.

Florizel stuck in the ice.

Many of the passengers had jammed the stairs with their luggage, all hoping, apparently, to make it to the lifeboats, and obviously unaware of the seriousness of the situation.

Great seas were smashing the entire length of the ship, sweeping human beings and luggage along with it as they emerged on the deck. The great majority of passengers were lost this way. Tons of water then began pouring down through the ship, sweeping people before it.

Ten minutes after she struck, the lights went out and blackness added to the chaos, and there followed a struggle for survival that brought forty-two people to safety and claimed the lives of ninety-four others.

There were many prominent business people on the *Florizel* this trip, including the managing director of the Red Cross Line, J. S. Munn and his little daughter Betty, and the well-known local mariner Captain Joe Kean was aboard as a passenger.

Shortly after she struck, Captain Kean was assisting with a lifeboat when a huge sea smashed into it. Some of the wreckage of the lifeboat hit Captain Kean and broke his leg. Alex Ledingham, Captain Martin, and Chief Officer James picked him up and assisted him to the smoking room where other passengers had gathered. Captain Kean thanked them but feared their efforts were futile. If he hadn't broken his leg he would stand a chance of surviving.

A short time later mountainous seas swept away the smoke room and the wheelhouse, taking with it about forty people in one fell swoop, including J.S. Munn and Captain Joe Kean.

Other passengers and crew trying to reach the front of the ship, which was still above water, were beaten and bruised by the seas until they were dazed and unconscious and then swept overboard.

One young man, whose name is to this day unknown, refused to help a woman, Miss Annie

Dalton, to a place of safety—she was drowned. Kitty Cantwell, the young woman who had asked him for assistance for her friend Annie, made it safely to the Marconi house after a sea swept her friend away.

A young pantry waiter, John Johnston, came across a passenger, Minnie Denief, and, fighting the sea, saved the young woman who was nearly swept away several times. Once she was swept over the rail and he grabbed her by the hair, hauling her back to safety.

A young serviceman, wounded at Gallipoli and travelling to New York with his wife and baby, tried valiantly to save his family as they beat their way to the Marconi room. A giant sea tore wife and baby from his arms and threw him, battered and bleeding, on the deck. He made it to the Marconi room eventually, but died shortly after.

Ninety-four lives were lost, many needlessly, for in their rush to get up top many people stepped from the shelter of the saloon to the unprotected deck which was being swamped by raging seas. They were swept overboard to their deaths in the twinkling of an eye.

A prominent city architect, W.F. Butler, his wife, and her brother-in-law, James J. McCoubrey, who had sheltered in the smoking room, tried to reach the Marconi room up forward. The three of them were seen by a survivor, hand in hand, attempting to reach the safety of the forward section, when a mountainous wave engulfed them and swept them to their deaths. John S. Munn was seen hanging onto a railing near the smoker in a dazed condition before he was swallowed up by the ocean.

Impaled amidships with a list to the starboard and buffeted by savage seas, the ship swung to and fro, making it even more difficult for survivors to move about, but forty-four survivors hung on with grim determination, many receiving severe bruises, cuts, and lacerations.

The Marconi room, which sheltered thirty-two of the survivors, was left standing only because the huge smokestack of the *Florizel* protected it from the full fury of the sea. Others found shelter on the fiddley (the grating and railing above the entrance to the stokehold) and in the forecastle.

Among the survivors crowding the little Marconi room were Captain Martin and Seaman Dooley. The captain had come to the decision that nothing could be done except perhaps try and get a line to shore, by tying a line to his waist and attempting to swim. In the event he drowned, at least his body would wash up on the shore and rescuers would have a line.

Seaman Dooley volunteered to swim ashore with him and both tried to reach forward to find a rope, but the seas were too powerful and the attempt had to be abandoned.

Then began the long, long wait for rescue. Messages from Cappahayden flashed back to St. John's about the wrecked liner, which sparked rescue operations immediately. Ships had to get up steam, crews had to be commandeered, and navy reservists from the HMS *Briton* were called upon to fill in. The *Prospero* was the first to leave port around midday.

Next, confusing messages began to arrive from Cappahayden to the effect that there were no survivors, all lives "had been lost," and the *Florizel* was a total wreck.

Rescue operations were halted and did not continue until more messages came from Cappahayden about sighting survivors on the wreckage. It was late afternoon before most of the ships steamed from St. John's to assist in the rescue operations, and it wasn't until daybreak on the following day that the ships reached the battered, broken *Florizel*.

The wreck of the SS *Florizel*. The smokestack protected the Marconi house, but the boat deck collapsed under the giant seas.

There were many acts of bravery by the rescue crews, but the storm was still at its height and it was impossible to get near the wreck.

Captain Perry of the *Gordon C* launched a dory and with Seaman Budden made four trips to the *Florizel*, taking off the two woman survivors first. On the fourth trip the raging seas overturned the dory, knocking the men semi-conscious.

Meantime, the other ships, SS *Home*, *Hawke*, and the *Terra Nova*, were having great difficulty launching their dories which kept capsizing, throwing the crews into the sea. An hour or more was spent fishing their own men from the sea and trying to keep the dories afloat.

Captain Nicholas Kennedy of the *Terra Nova* had called for two volunteers to man the whaling dory with him, and two seamen, W.H. Clouter and G.H. Penney, volunteered. They rescued Seaman Budden, when others thought he had drowned, and took him back to his ship. Captain Perry, given up for lost, was also rescued by the *Terra Nova* whaling dory and deposited, unconscious, aboard the *Home*.

Fearing any further loss of life, the ships lay off and waited for the storm to abate somewhat before attempting any further rescue.

Presently there was a lull in the gale, and again Clouter and Penney begged to go to the rescue with Captain Kennedy. The three of them got into the sturdy dory and made for the *Florizel*. Five times the dory capsized, but she was unsinkable, and five times the men righted her, clambered aboard, and kept rowing for the wreck. They finally got under the lee of the *Florizel* and took off twenty-five survivors.

Other ships also got their dories out and, after a good hour's battle with the elements, with great difficulty, made it to the lee side of the *Florizel*, and soon all survivors were removed.

One survivor, Major Sullivan, a hefty man well over 200 pounds, missed the dory when he jumped and landed in the sea. Marine Engineer Alex Ledingham caught the major and held on to him. The major was towed a considerable distance, when Captain Simonsen of the *Hawke* manoeuvred a dory in such a way, tipped it on its side, and rolled the major into it.

These were but a few of the brave acts that came to light, for it was impossible to keep track of all that was going on at the time. Captain Kennedy delivered his survivors to the *Prospero* where doctors were waiting to look after them.

The lull then passed and the storm continued with unabated fury so that any effort to save the *Florizel* had to be abandoned. The following day in comparative calm, the *Terra Nova* returned to the *Florizel* and recovered seven bodies in the wreck.

Captain Kennedy cited three of his men for bravery to the British Admiralty after it was finished. They were W.H. Clouter, a member of the *Terra Nova*'s crew, and W.H. Penney and A. Morey, naval reservists of the HMS *Briton*.

In the lengthy inquiry that followed, the cause for the wreck of the *Florizel* was laid to gale-force winds, ice, poor visibility, and the possibility of the Arctic current reversing itself on that particular night, thus further impeding the speed of the ship.

There was much speculation that the captain had been under pressure at the time to leave port in spite of the impending storm, but this he denied.

Captain William Martin was suspended for twenty-one months, but in view of his previous good record and general care and attention to duty, was allowed a Chief Mate's Interim Certificate for the time suspension.

Today at Bowring Park in St. John's, Newfoundland, visitors can view a statue of Peter Pan,

The Peter Pan monument in Bowring Park, St. John's, Newfoundland. Erected in memory of Betty Munn, victim of the SS *Florizel* disaster. It was unveiled on August 29, 1925, and reads, "In memory of a little girl who loved the park."

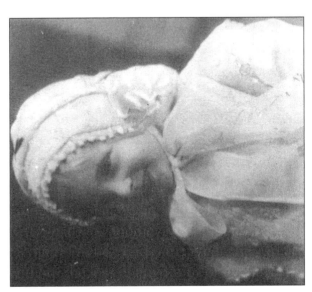

Betty Munn, shown here, was torn from her father's arms as he struggled to reach safety from the monstrous waves on the deck of the stricken SS *Florizel*, shipwrecked at Cappahayden, Newfoundland.

erected by the Munn family. It is dedicated to little Betty Munn and stands as a memorial to all the victims of the SS *Florizel* disaster.

The FLORIZEL *Disaster*

KITTY CANTWELL'S STORY

Mrs. Mike McDonald doesn't think too much about it these days because the memory of the wreck of the *Florizel* has not been a pleasant one. She does recall it as a terrible experience and it ended her hopes of ever seeing a bit of the world before she settled down.

Kitty Cantwell was going to visit her sister in New York that winter and was eager to see some of the United States before her marriage to Mike McDonald, and it was a happy young girl who boarded the *Florizel* that Saturday, February 23, 1918.

Kitty's travelling companion was her good friend, Miss Annie Dalton of Western Bay, who was also going to New York, to take up a position in a clothing factory.

It was a nasty night when the *Florizel* left the port of St. John's. When she was an hour out of port a south-east gale and snowstorm came on, and continued until midnight when the wind chopped around to the east-northeast and blew with violence

Kitty's good friend, Annie, got seasick, but Kitty didn't mind the rolling of the ship at all. She actually enjoyed the rough motion of the *Florizel* as she pitched through rough seas and, still greatly excited about the whole trip, she was unable to sleep.

She was wide awake when the *Florizel* impaled itself on Horn Head Point off Cappahayden on the Southern Shore at dawn.

In the roar and confusion that followed, Kitty got her friend up and dressed. Then, as they left their stateroom, the lights went out.

Clinging together, they were swept along by the seas rushing in through the broken ship. It was Kitty who encouraged her friend along, for Annie was still weak and shaken from her bout of seasickness.

Pushed and battered by the heavy seas, the two girls were carried along, Kitty grabbing whatever her hands found and Annie clinging to her.

The after part of the ship was submerged beneath the heavy seas and she was fast disintegrating. People were swept overboard, disappearing in the huge waves swamping the ship. Kitty was grimly concerned with survival as she and Annie worked their way to the fore of the ship which was still above sea level.

A young stalwart appeared beside them and Kitty appealed to him for help for Annie, but he said he couldn't help and soon disappeared from their view in the combers sweeping the ship. Kitty didn't know if he survived or not.

They were nearing safety, the Marconi room up ahead of them, when a huge wave caught Annie Dalton off balance and swept her overboard.

Kitty found herself alone, crawling on her hands and knees across the deck to the door of the Marconi room. She pounded on it and called out, demanding to be let in.

At first a voice called back that it was all filled, but another voice cried, "It's a woman, let her in!"

As she huddled resignedly outside, the door opened and someone pulled her in to safety.

There were twenty-two other survivors in the tiny room, a precarious shelter spared only because the huge smokestack of the ship took the brunt of the huge, savage seas.

Altogether, forty-two people survived the disaster, including one other woman besides Kitty. Her name was Minnie Denief.

Daily News reporter Cassie Brown, shown here, interviews Kitty Cantwell about her harrowing experience on the SS *Florizel*, shipwrecked in 1918 on the Southern Shore of Newfoundland.

Kitty never did get to New York. She married Mike McDonald a few months later, cured of her desire to travel. From that day on, relatives in the United States could not get her to travel to visit them.

Tragedy At St. Jacques Island

THE KATHERINE FIANDER STORY

The Christmas of 1963 was one of tragedy as a three-day storm battered the Atlantic Provinces and took the lives of twenty-eight men. In the ocean surrounding Newfoundland, six of the seven-man crew of the 124-ton Newfoundland coastal freighter *Mary Pauline* were lost when the vessel sank in mountainous seas off St. Pierre and Miquelon; twelve crew members of the French freighter *Douala* were lost a little farther up the coast off Burgeo, and two other Newfoundlanders were swept into the sea from the Island of St. Jacques.

The two men swept into the sea were Eric Fiander and Hughie Myles, lightkeepers on St. Jacques Island. They disappeared at the beginning of the three-day storm and left a young woman to keep a lonely vigil with her three small babies for three bitter, frightful days.

Katherine Fiander had been married for five years. Her twenty-six-year-old husband, Eric, and their three small babies: Alton, three; John, two; and

Karen, one, were happy and cozy in the residence of the lighthouse at St. Jacques Island, a small rocky island less than a mile from the mainland on the south coast of Newfoundland.

Ariel photo of St. Jacques Island.

Eric was the assistant lightkeeper. He was in charge, since the head keeper, Hubert Myles, was ashore on leave. Meanwhile, Hubert's nephew, seventeen-year-old Hughie Myles, was also on the island to help Eric.

The island itself is less than a mile in length and is roughly shaped like a horseshoe; the cliff bridging the middle is less than 175 yards in width.

The residence was approximately 200 yards from the lighthouse and the whistle, on the outer tip of the island facing the Atlantic. In a small building by itself, apart from the residence, was the diesel generator which supplied electricity to the residence, lighthouse, and whistle. During this particular period the generator had to be started by hand with a crank because of weakening batteries. New batteries were somewhere along the way but had not yet arrived.

Contact with the mainland was maintained by water, and a shed housing the Department of Transport's boat's engine and other equipment was on the strip of beach on the other side of the island. Contact was also made twice daily with the DOT station at Burin, through radio-telephone, at 10:30 A.M. and 8:30 P.M.

The residence itself was heated by a hard-coal furnace, with additional heat coming from the kitchen oil range. The oil drum connected to the stove was on the back of the house, but the main supply of oil was near the whistle house, 200 yards away. As a precautionary measure in stormy weather, a lifeline spanned the distance between the residence and lighthouse.

The storm struck on Thursday night, December 19, and by Friday was raging in all its fury with winds gusting up to 100 miles per hour when contact was made with the DOT station in Burin, at 10:30 that morning, by Eric Fiander.

The men then made their rounds, checking the lighthouse, whistle, and the shed on the beach. They returned to the house dinnertime with the news that the shed was being blown over, and decided that as soon as they had finished dinner they would return to the beach with a rope to secure it.

They left immediately after dinner, and Katherine had her hands full with the children and the housework until three o'clock when she heard Eric call, "Katherine!"

Above the whine of the wind his voice sounded as if it came from the basement, and as she was fully occupied with the small children at that moment, she didn't answer.

He called again, louder this time, "*Katherine!*"

She called back, "What?"

He did not reply. She kept doing what she had been doing for a few moments, then grew suddenly alert and frightened. Had she heard Eric calling, or was it the wind?

She listened uneasily for a moment to the howling wind, then gave herself a mental shake. *Of course it was Eric*, she told herself. She had heard him call her name twice.

She gave the basement a hurried check but found no sign of her husband or his young helper, and a nagging fear took possession of her. She decided firmly that it had been the wind and not his voice after all...even if she knew she had heard him call her.

She worked about the house, keeping her hands busy and her eyes glued to the window facing the island, watching for a glimpse of the men. Her ears were alert for other sounds than that of the wind and sea, but the afternoon passed and still the men hadn't returned.

Now fear was growing, but she would not give in to it. She made many excuses for their continued absence. Perhaps the cliff was too icy for them to climb; perhaps they were staying in the shed until the worst of the storm was over; perhaps...

When the men did not return for supper, Katherine Fiander changed her thinking and forced herself to admit that something must have gone wrong. Perhaps, she reasoned, Eric had been hurt and decided to remain in the shed...

She would think no further than that.

Now a problem presented itself to Katherine. With daylight going she had no light in the house, and the lighthouse had no light unless she could go out to the generator and get it started, but one look at the lifeline changed her mind. Ice six inches thick coated the lifeline, and ocean spray had also coated the ground with slick, treacherous ice. To try to cross that stretch to the shed in the half-light would be suicide in that hurricane.

Black night descended, bringing no relief from the fury of the storm, serving only to heighten its intensity. There was no friendly light shining from the residence window and no warning light emanating from the lighthouse. All was in darkness. With no generator there could be no contact with the DOT stations, either.

Katherine had put the two smaller children to bed but let three-year-old Alton stay up to keep her company, and the two sat in the kitchen, which was lit only by the flickering light of the oil stove. Alton's endless chatter was, for the first time, a godsend.

Later, after little Alton finally went off to bed and to sleep, Katherine found the house growing cold. A hurried check showed her the kitchen stove was out; a further check revealed that the furnace, too, was completely out. In her anxiety about the men she had forgotten to keep the furnace stoked. The oil tank for the kitchen stove must have emptied, too, and she was now without heat as well as light.

Katherine Fiander kept a long, lonely vigil that night, her mind full of fears for her man and for Hughie Myles as she paced endlessly. The storm hadn't slacked at all when daybreak came.

She tried to light the furnace, but could not get the hard coal to ignite. The men had always started the furnace by throwing stove oil on the hard coal, but there was not a drop of oil in the house. It was all in the tank 200 yards away, and the system used by the men to transfer it to the tank attached to the kitchen stove involved a pump and hose too cumbersome and complicated for Katherine who had never bothered with those things.

Later, as the last vestige of heat left the house, Katherine dressed and, grasping the ice-coated lifeline, made it somehow to the shed where she began to work on the generator as she had seen the men work on it. If she could get the generator working she could get heat from the hot plates, the iron, and the electric kettle, and she would have warm food for her children.

Snow had seeped into the shed and covered the now cold and weak batteries. When Katherine tried to start the generator with the hand crank it gave not a gig. She didn't know it, but there were compression levers to pull as well before the engine would start.

A strength greater than hers was needed to get the generator going and, at last, her arms aching with the strain, she gave up and fought her way back to the residence. By now she had the children dressed in every bit of heavy clothing they had, and she worked about the house, feeding the children cold meals, keeping her hands busy, answering the numberless questions little Alton put to her because it kept her mind off the future.

One certainty she still resisted. *Eric will be all right,* she told herself.

The second day was passing with no let-up in the storm and, thrown upon her own resources, she searched the house for something, anything, that might give them light for the long, black night ahead. She found an old kerosene lamp with a broken flue and enough oil to give a tiny light during the night.

Katherine passed the second night without food or rest. She hadn't eaten a morsel since the men had left the residence after dinner on Friday, nor had she rested or slept. She felt neither hungry nor tired as the second night passed, but alert and confident and full of hope that somehow Eric and Hughie were still alive.

Just before dawn on Sunday the wind stopped and the silence was frightening. She waited in silence, listening for the fall of a footstep, for anything to indicate that there was life on the island outside the residence.

Then it was dawn, and dawn showed a brilliantly beautiful day. It was as if the fury and havoc of the three preceding nights had never happened. Katherine went outside, her eyes searching the island, and now another fear took possession of her. Supposing she went to the shed to look for the men and they weren't there?

This fine, calm Sunday was not so pleasant now, and while her eyes scoured the cliffs where Eric and Hughie might appear, she was a woman afraid to the core of her being. She was afraid to go to the shed because Eric might not be there. As long as she did not know for sure, she could hope, and hope was the only thing that kept her from going to pieces.

Later, she saw two men coming along the cliff toward the house and for a fleeting moment thought it was Eric and Hughie, but in the same moment she recognized two friends, Tom Osbourne and Roland Stoodly from Coombs Cove, and in that split-second she accepted the inevitable, that Eric was gone forever and she had known it all along—from the moment she had heard him call her name.

As the two men came up to the residence, the self-control she had exercised for three days deserted her. She ran to them, screaming at the top of her lungs, "Eric and Hughie are gone!"

They had seen no sign of Eric or Hughie either.

On the beach, high-water marks showed that the seas had gone right up the cliffs behind the shed, and it was evident that the waves had swept both men away while they were trying to secure the small building.

As she left the island that same day, Katherine's eyes swept the beach, searching the base of the cliff, hoping she might see Eric or Hughie. They might have been too weak or cold to reach home, but they might be still alive, she thought, in one last, vain outburst of hope. Her eyes were still riveted to the island as her friends took her into Coombs Cove.

Wedding photo. L-R: Ward Harris and Rose Harris of Rose Blanche; Eric Fiander; Katherine (Harris) Fiander.

Hughie's body was recovered on the beach on Monday, but Eric Fiander's body was never found. The sea claimed him and never gave him back.

Tragedy followed Katherine Fiander, who returned to her own family in Rose Blanche that summer of 1964, then settled in nearby Harbour le Cou. It was discovered after her ordeal that another baby was on the way. On September 13, another son was born to Katherine, and she named him Eric Bruce. On October 22, baby Eric died in his sleep.

While a December storm raged outside, Katherine Fiander and her three small children spent two frightful nights alone in the lightkeeper's house on St. Jacques Island, Newfoundland. Without heat or light, and cut off from all communication from the mainland, she could not know that the storm which kept them trapped on the island had taken the lives of her husband, Eric, and his assistant, Hughie Myles.

Mutiny on the
SS _Diana_

It isn't often that one hears of mutiny on the high seas in reference to Newfoundland seamen, but mutiny did occur in the spring of 1922 during the annual seal hunt, and the mutineers burned the ship to boot. The ship was the _Diana_, under command of Captain John Parsons.

Newspaper reports of the day merely stated that the _Diana_ had been disabled and, after drifting among the ice floes about twelve days, had been abandoned by her crew. The reports also stated, "It is understood that before leaving the doomed ship she was set on fire and went down during the day."

A well-known Newfoundland adventurer, Jack Dodd, was a sealer on the _Diana_ on her last memorable trip to the icefields, and it is through his story we learn of the mutiny and unnecessary end of the stout ship _Diana_.

Mr. Dodd's story is corroborated by American writer George Allan England, who also went to the seal hunt that year on Bowring's ship the _Terra Nova_ and, in his book _Vikings of the Ice_, published in 1924, references are made to the _Diana_ and the mutiny.

Jack Dodd was twenty years old that spring, and he was a happy young man to get a coveted berth on the stout oaken ship, but the *Diana* seemed to be dogged by bad luck right from the beginning. She had no sooner gotten off from Torbay when eight stowaways were discovered and the ship had to return to port. This was a bad omen, the crew felt.

Their fears seemed justified when after this delay the *Diana* left the harbour to find she had to take an easterly course because a change in the wind had brought the ice close to land. On top of that, the crew discovered they had a jinker — a person blamed for bad luck — on board.

After butting her way through heavy ice with help from the sealers, who heaved her along with a hawser and the help of dynamite, the *Diana* made it safely to the icefields.

Sleet, snow, frost, and gales of wind kept the crew busy. George Allan England noted in his book that the *Terra Nova*, under Captain Abram Kean, was as usual leading the fleet with the *Thetis*, under Captain Billy Winsor, and the *Diana* dogging their every "jibe and cut."

Author England wrote, "So close *Thetis* pressed that collision threatened. It came to collision too; not serious, but at all events we carried off one of her boats — where at indignant yells from her, derisive laughter from us. Well, good luck anyhow: *Thetis* was to some extent crippled."

Mike Murphy of St. John's, a staffer at *The Daily News*, was cabin boy on the *Thetis* that spring, and, if his recollections are correct, it was collision with a growler (a baby iceberg) that staved in the bow of the *Thetis*.

On March 14, the *Diana* was well among the white-coats, and on the fifteenth, the day the seal hunt officially opened, thousands of seals were killed, "It was like a charge on a battlefield," Jack Dodd said.

Three days later, near-tragedy occurred shortly after the *Diana* started killing whitecoats. On this day, Jack and a number of his mates became marooned on a large pan of ice which broke away from the main body and, at nightfall, with the temperature dropping to zero, snowing and blowing, they were still marooned and the *Diana* was not to be seen.

There were twenty-one of them in the group, a number of them friends of Jack's from Torbay. There was Francis Whitty, James and George Bradbury, Allan Codner, and Joseph Martin, to name a few, and, of course, there was the "jinker."

The master watch, Kenneth Snow of Bay Roberts, kept the men moving constantly. They had tried to light a fire by burning their gaffs, but the gaffs were made of green wood and were too green to burn.

It was bitterly cold, and the master watch kept them moving. He made them do the "American eight," then "round the house," keeping them constantly on the move.

There was talk among them of another *Greenland* or *Newfoundland* disaster and, when some men became discouraged and sat down on the ice, Kenneth Snow kept after them, made them get up and keep moving. All through the cold, bitter hours they moved around and around on their ice pan, wondering why the *Diana* wasn't looking for them. They were on the edge of a lake of open water and found it difficult to understand why no one was searching for them.

It was between three and four o'clock in the morning when they saw the lights of a ship opposite them, and they cheered and shouted thinking it was their ship. It was not the *Diana* but the *Thetis*, looking for two of her own men still on the ice.

Incredibly, the *Thetis* did not stop to pick up the *Diana*'s men. Captain Winsor called down to *Diana*'s master watch, telling him he'd be back shortly, that he had to pick up a couple of his own men farther down the lake. "Don't worry, I know where you are. The *Diana* is jammed; she can't get to you. But don't worry, we'll be back."

Said Jack Dodd, "We thought it funny at the time. We were ready to go aboard, but the way the tide was running we knew the 'lake' would remain open and he'd be back."

Sure enough, a short time later the *Thetis* returned and picked them up, and Captain Winsor ordered liberal doses of rum for the half-frozen sealers. Said Jack, "I didn't have to be rocked asleep that night!"

At seven o'clock the following morning Captain Winsor dropped the twenty-one sealers on the ice and gave them the direction of the *Diana*. She was not to be seen on the horizon, but about 3:00 P.M. they walked aboard their own ship.

However, the *Diana*'s troubles were just about to begin. She got clear of the ice jam only to become stuck again a short time later and the sealers were once again called upon to heave on the line. Eighty men hauled away on the towline until 8:00 P.M. but had to give up and go aboard.

Meantime, about 8,000 seals were stowed in the hold of the *Diana* and it looked like they were going to have a bumper crop. There was even the possibility of an early trip back to St. John's. It was not to be, for as the *Diana* continued to butt her way through the heavy ice her propeller struck a growler, which broke the main shaft. This happened on the eve of St. Patrick's Day, and for the *Diana* it was the beginning of the end.

This very same night was one fraught with anxiety, for the tide pressed the ice together so hard it began to raft up around the ship, and sheet after sheet came in over the deck. The sealers worked frantically, chopping and throwing chunks of ice over the ship's side. Finally the ice stopped coming aboard, but it nipped the *Diana* under the keel and pushed her right up on top of the ice. High and dry, the *Diana* went over gently on her side. "So gently she wouldn't break an eggshell," Jack Dodd said.

The *Diana* lay over as far as she could go, completely out of the water, so the crew took to the ice, some of them even taking their luggage. In the distance they could see the lights of the *Thetis*, but since Captain Parsons remained on the bridge and would not give the order to abandon ship, the sealers drifted back to the *Diana*.

By morning, the *Diana* was still on top of the ice and the crew could see that two of her planks were splintered on her starboard side, leaving a hole near the engine room. This meant she would likely go to the bottom when the ice loosened and she settled in the water again.

However, Captain Parsons refused to give the order to abandon ship, and, that afternoon when the ice began to slacken, the sealers, with their belongings, waited for the verdict, on the ice.

The *Diana* settled back in the sea as the ice loosened and the word was passed around that the ship was leaking badly but could be kept afloat with pumps. So the die was cast.

On March 18, the disabled *Diana* could keep afloat with her pumps, but her engines could not help her in any other way with her shaft broken. She would now have to depend on her canvas for manoeuvrability.

It was on this day that the sealers saw rats deserting the *Diana*. Said Jack, "It was brought to my attention, and when we went up we could see quite a few rats and two or three small ones, and we figured those rats were headed for the *Thetis*." The *Thetis*, meanwhile, was now out of sight of the *Diana* in the wheeling ice. The sight of the rats leaving the ship caused great discontent among the men. Later that day a gale of northeast wind brought frost and snow. It was so bitter and frosty the men could not face it.

Now the *Diana* was in the greatest peril, for the ice was breaking up around her. Since she was powerless to control her movements, she was rolling and pitching between the ice which would have caved her in but for her stout oaken beams. She was running before the wind with the aid of a few pieces of canvas on her yardarms for'ard and was moving for the safety of the heavier ice a few miles ahead, when a huge iceberg loomed suddenly. At the mercy of the wind and tide, the *Diana* blew right into the ice mass, her rigging tangling into an arm of ice protruding from the berg. There was a great crash as the yardarm broke.

The *Diana*, caught fast by the rigging, listed to the port and swung round and round. Men ran with axes to chop away the ice-arm but were ordered to stop by the captain, who feared the iceberg might topple on them. As it was, huge lumps of ice were falling to the deck and the men had to duck for protection.

The *Diana* was well and truly caught by the iceberg, the ropes and wires of the yardarm were tangled around the pinnacle of ice, and here Jack Dodd did a brave but foolish thing for which he received no thanks. He shinnied up the rigging, scrambled out on the yardarm and, with his knife, cut through the ropes that held the ship to the berg. As he cut through the last strand the yardarm gave way beneath his feet, but he grabbed a rope and swung to safety.

The *Diana* gave a great roll to starboard and floated free of the iceberg, and as she rolled back, the frame holding the *Diana*'s ten lifeboats (all set into one another) came in contact with the arm of ice that had held her prisoner and shattered all the boats. But the ship was free.

Now the sealers were more discontented than ever. Not only was their ship disabled and leaking, but if anything further should happen, they didn't have a boat to keep them afloat—not that the puny little boats would have been much help, the older sealers told the younger men.

Clear of that first iceberg, the *Diana* was drifting down a stretch of broken ice and running before the wind. Her canvas was laid on and then lowered, depending on the drift of the wind and sea as she sought the safety of the heavier ice.

For the next three days the *Diana* followed a pattern that kept the crew jittery and wondering if the next minute would be their last. She had drifted among a city of icebergs (Jack counted 110 of them), and Captain Parsons and his crew were kept alert and busy manoeuvring the ship through them. There were times when the gallant ship could not avoid the bergs.

Said Jack, "We'd drift down on the iceberg right easy, rub up against it, and our foremast rigging would catch on the jutting peaks of the berg. All the men would stand clear and take cover while she worked herself free, for great hunks of ice would drop off the berg to her deck."

Sometimes, *Diana* was caught by the foremast, other times by the mizzen-mast. Sometimes she was really "clinched" to the berg and she'd swing around and back and forth, and the captain had to keep a strict eye on the men to see that they did not try to run up the rigging, as Jack had done, and try to cut her free. This practice, he informed them, not only endangered a life, it endangered *all* their lives, so no matter how long it took, *Diana* had to work herself free.

The strain was terrific.

When the ice was loose and broken and the seas were rough and loppy, the winds would heave the *Diana* on an iceberg and she'd scrape and grind along as the iceberg would take her, roll her up and down like a dog worrying a bone, until the water and hunks of ice came in over her sides.

They escaped most of the bergs by manipulating the sails and yardarms, and Captain Parsons was on the bridge constantly, on guard for the safety of his ship. The *Diana* tangled with five icebergs altogether. Some of them did no damage, but the others pretty well limbed her out. The foremast and the mizzen-mast took the beatings; some of the rigging was torn out of the bulwarks and just hung from the mast, but while the masts took the worst of the strain, they didn't break or splinter.

George Allan England made note of the many icebergs. He wrote, "They jostle us, we elbow them."

The sealing vessel SS *Diana*, abandoned in the ice off Newfoundland in 1922.

Meantime, *Diana*'s crew were beginning to murmur aloud. It seemed unreasonable to them that they should be expected to drift about the icefields day after day, banging into icebergs and being generally beaten about by the ice, and they demanded that an SOS be sent out.

It was then that word was sent from the bridge that help was on the way, and the men felt easier.

Now the *Diana* became jammed again, and there was a shortage of drinking water. Ice from the bergs had to be melted, and it was passed from bloody, greasy mitt to mitt, and was hardly fit for human consumption when it was melted down.

The days passed and still there was no sign of rescue. The *Diana* was constantly being ground between the tight ice and her men were exhausted from trying to heave her bodily through the ice with a towline. Mutiny was the topic of the day, because Captain Parsons refused point-blank to send out an SOS.

Actually, arrangements had been made by her owners (Baird's) for the *Sable Island I* to go after her and tow her back to port. A couple of days later, these plans had been changed and arrangements had been made to have the SS *Watchful* sent to her assistance and have the *Diana* towed to port as soon as the ice loosened. Other ships at the icefields were aware of *Diana*'s troubles but were unable to get to her. Also, they didn't particularly make an attempt since she seemed to be in no immediate danger.

The men were fed up. They felt their lives were in danger every moment they remained aboard the *Diana* and, when the master watch, Kenneth Snow told them,

"Boys, it's getting serious, we want an SOS sent out, we should insist," they were ready to do so.

There was a lot of loud talk then, and a bunch of the sealers who were war veterans began to spoil for a fight. There was talk about getting the captain and throwing him overboard if he didn't send out an SOS. However, Captain Parsons didn't scare very easily, and it was reported to the sealers that he sent out a warning that the first man who came for him would be shot.

George Allan England reports in his book, *Vikings Of The Ice*, an interview he had with an officer of the *Diana*. The officer told him that the mutineers had five rifles for'ard and, if someone would make the balls, the mutineers would fire them. The rest of the rifles were aft with the captain and his crew.

A delegation of forty men came aft and it got ugly. They said they'd bust up the Marconi house and throw the captain and the Marconi operator overboard if they didn't send out an SOS.

One particular officer of the *Diana* said the ship was only leaking six inches in four hours and *Diana* could have kept afloat easily. Meantime, he had rigged a hose to give the mutineers a shot of steam if his captain ordered it. The captain didn't, and after some haranguing, he gave in to the sealers, who marched to the Marconi room and ordered the SOS sent out. After that, twelve of the mutineers were left to guard the Marconi operator.

Jack Dodd states that the *Diana* was leaking three thousand gallons an hour. He further states that Captain Parsons did *not* consent to sending out an SOS, that the sealers themselves, in an ugly mood, took over the Marconi room.

The SS *Sagona*. The crew of the ill-fated SS *Diana* transfer their belongs to the rescue ship SS *Sagona* before abandoning their ship altogether.

The SOS was picked up by the SS *Seal* and the SS *Sagona*, and the latter began to steam for the *Diana*. She did not reach her until the following evening, and while all ships of the icefields learned that the *Diana*'s crews had mutinied not a word of it seemed to have leaked to the press in St. John's.

Now that the sealers were abandoning the *Diana* and since she was still so jammed she could not be towed, her owners gave her up as lost. Orders were given to the captain to open the seacocks of the gallant ship and let her sink.

Captain Parsons offered the captain and crew of the Sagona anything they could salvage off the *Diana* before she went down and *Sagona*'s Captain Job Knee decided that among other things, he would like to have the seal pelts already stowed in the *Diana*, but only a few hundred had been removed when there was the shout of "Fire!" — The mutineers, not wanting the *Sagona*'s crew to have their pelts, set fire to the *Diana*.

That was the end of the *Diana*, a stout and gallant ship that had withstood the incredible batterings of the Arctic ice floes to the end. Her captain left her reluctantly and only when he had no alternative.

The *Diana* fought hard to live and she died hard. Jack Dodd said, "She burned to the water's rim. She had started to settle and had gone down headfirst, but when we thought she was gone, she came up again, the forward part of her still blazing. She seemed to straighten but then she went stern first and the last we saw of her was her bow protruding — then there was an explosion.

Perhaps because the gallant ship had taken them safely through so much in the preceding twelve days, Jack actually wept as the *Diana* went down. "Don't ask me why I cried, but I felt that it was like someone belonging to me was getting buried," he said.

The *Diana*'s officer who told George Allan England about the mutiny was still angry when interviewed in St. John's weeks later. "It was a bloody crime the way she was burned, her and all them thousands of sculps. Yes sir, a bloody crime."

The LEICASTER

SAVED BY NEWFOUNDLANDERS

Undoubtedly, one of the most awesome sights ever
seen at sea is a ship on her beam ends. When a ship
in this condition drifts about the Atlantic and
survives three hurricanes, she becomes a bit of a
phenomenon.

There was such a ship! Her name was the *Leicester*,
and she was eventually towed to port by a crew of
Newfoundlanders working on the salvage tug
Foundation Josephine and her crew would share a
harrowing adventure.

The *Leicester* had left London for New York,
September 4, 1948. On September 14, when she was
about 300 miles southeast of Cape Race, her radio
stopped receiving and she was unable to hear the
hurricane warnings that cleared the shipping lanes
rapidly. The *Leicester* found herself in the middle of the
hurricane, and at its height, her ballast of sand and
gravel shifted. She rolled over to a fifty-five-degree
list—and stayed there. She was still afloat, listing to
seventy degrees when she rolled, and her crew abandoned her.

A couple of days later the *Leicester* was reported still afloat and the Foundation Maritime Ltd., Halifax, sent two of their tugs after the prize — the *Foundation Josephine* and the *Foundation Lillian*. One of the Newfoundlanders on the *Josie* (as she was affectionately called by her crew) was Dave Clarke of Harbour le Cou.

Dave Clarke of Harbour le Cou was one of the Newfoundlanders aboard the salvage tug *Foundation Josephine* when she recovered the *Leicester*, victim of three hurricanes!

The two tugs scoured the ocean in the vicinity where she had last been reported, but could find no sign of the *Leicester*, and after a couple of days, came to the conclusion that she had gone down. Meantime, an ancient Greek freighter, the *Orion*, had gone hard aground and caught fire at Flower's Cove in the Strait of Belle Isle, and the *Josie* was directed there to save the old ship.

The *Leicester* was forgotten and the *Josie* steamed for the *Orion*, and worked on her for two days, but "she was too far gone," Dave Clarke recalled. A storm was brewing and seas began to batter the wreck which had some of the *Josie*'s crew on board.

They were abandoning her when a message from the company in Halifax notified them that the *Leicester* had been seen drifting off the Azores: *Josie* and *Lillian* were to get to her fast!

The second hurricane was brewing and the *Josie* steamed right into it, but even this powerful tug "hove to" for about seven or eight hours to ride out the storm. "It was a couple of bad days going down to the Azores," said Dave Clarke.

It was the *Lillian* that found the *Leicester* ten days after she had been abandoned. She came upon the *Leicester* on the evening of September 26, while the *Josie* arrived on the scene at dawning of the following day.

Said Dave Clarke, "The *Leicester* was a hard sight to see, listed out bad with a 55 degree list—she was just like a boat hove over the wharf under paint, you could almost walk on her broadside."

The *Josie* circled the ship and Mr. Clarke said the sharks were "as thick as maggots."

The *Josie*'s crew got to work immediately and boarded the *Leicester* with great difficulty because of the steep slant of her deck. When she rolled, her rail went under and she kept taking water through the doors that had been left open. The crew of the *Josie* closed the doors and proceeded to attach the towline.

"The sharks were so thick, they used to cut the ropes," said Mr. Clarke. "We hauled in the log line that *Leicester* was trailing and found a shark attached to the log at the end of it!"

Dave Clarke, and the mate, Wally Miles, with the aid of three other Newfoundlanders, made fast the towline, and by noon *Josie* had the *Leicester* under way.

It was a hard tow job. *Leicester*'s rudder was jammed hard a-port and she kept sheering and rolling until her bridge touched the water. On board the *Josie* her crew was ready to part the towline in case the *Leicester* did take the plunge. The *Lillian* brought up to the rear of the big ship.

Josie was ordered to take her tow to New York, but the order was later changed and they headed for Bermuda, arriving there a week later. She was anchored at Coney Island, Bermuda, in a shallow harbour that had little or no protection from the elements.

Josie's crew were put to work shifting the ballast to get *Leicester* upright again. Said Dave Clarke, "we were three days dumping ballast, and we had to burn a hole in the side of her so we could shovel it out through."

After days of shovelling, the ship's list was greatly reduced and *Leicester* was considered safe enough to go into St. George's harbour, seven miles away, so her owners could claim her, but the third and the worst hurricane of all was brewing and there was no time for the ships to get out of the shallow harbour.

The *Josie*'s crew battened down the *Leicester* and their own ship, attached their tug to the *Leicester* and prepared to ride out the storm.

The hurricane made headlines in Newfoundland, killed people, injured hundreds and caused millions of dollars worth of damage along the Florida coastline.

The hurricane hit the unprotected harbour, churning the shallow waters until they boiled furiously, *Josie* snapping her mooring lines like so much thread—her anchor chain also snapped and sent the sturdy tug smashing into the *Leicester*'s side. *Josie*'s own steel plates buckled under the impact and she began to leak.

The captain decided that their only hope of survival was to get out to sea, but, as Dave Clarke said, "I was at the wheel and we had a helluva time getting clear of the *Leicester*. When we did, the *Josie* wouldn't come to the wind."

The *Josie* received a battering such as she had never received before. Her lifeboats were wrenched away and her aerial blew off as Dave Clarke wrestled with the ship and tried to bring her around. "But we had to go where the wind carried us. She couldn't slew up to it at all. She never come up but three degrees, even with five hundred horsepower, and I had her hard over," he said.

They could see nothing for the wild seas and torrential rain, and no one could tell where they were. It was impossible to stay on deck due to the wind, which was gusting up to 120 miles per hour.

It grew dark as *Josie* was beaten mercilessly by the waves. Dave Clarke was still trying to get her to head into the wind when she struck something on the bottom. As he remembers it, "*Josie* beat over a ridge of rock until she brought up on the far edge."

She hung there on the edge of a reef with her bow hanging over deep water, and in the pitch-black night no one could see if they had hit one of the myriad of reefs offshore or if she had driven ashore.

Below deck, *Josie* was full of water, and if she slid off the reef she would go down like a rock. There was nothing to do but wait it out.

A couple of hours later the seas began to abate a little and wind began to drop, although it was still raining and stormy. With the aid of flashlights the men began to probe the darkness surrounding them.

Was that land?

The captain spoke up. "Who's going to see?"

Dave Clarke said, "I'll go, Cap'n."

The captain ordered a rope tied beneath Dave's arms. "We won't let you drown, Dave. We'll haul you back."

Surf roared on the rocks around *Josie*, and when it receded Dave jumped, lighting his way through the spume with a flashlight. "We won't lose you, Dave," the captain shouted.

Between spray and surf Dave could see another rock beyond the one *Josie* was on, and he jumped for it. At that moment he didn't know there was at least thirty-five feet of water beneath him, but he landed safely. With his flashlight he could see a ridge of land leading to the mainland.

He yelled back to the captain, "We're on dry land. We're on the mainland, sir. Give me another man."

In a few minutes young Albert Green of Burgeo appeared on the land beside him. He carried a line to hold the ship fast to the land so that they might rig a bos'n's chair. "But we just got the line around a boulder when a great sea picked up *Josie* and hove her right up against land, and there she was, right snug, " said Dave Clarke.

The rest of the crew could step off the *Josie* right onto land!

Daybreak revealed the *Josie* as a complete wreck. Of the *Leicester* there wasn't a sign, until somebody spotted her less than half a mile from *Josie*. The *Leicester* too had been driven ashore and was lying snug against the land.

Although the *Foundation Josephine* was a wreck and well in over the reef, she was patched up and hauled off and put in dry dock, but not before the *Leicester* was refloated and brought safely into the deep harbour of St. George's where she underwent repairs.

Said Dave, "That was my last time on the *Josie*. They fixed her up and carried her over to England. Her five-year lease with the Foundation Company was at an end."

Dave Clarke is an active sixty-nine-year-old seaman who looks a good ten years younger than his age. He had been going to sea since his early teens and was master of a ship by the time he was eighteen. Like most Newfoundland seamen, he was rum-running for four years in the days of prohibition.

He has stayed with the sea all his life, and at the age of sixty-nine he is still looking for a ship.

The Loss of the HOPE

At nine o'clock on the morning of September 22, 1921, the vessel *Hope*, under sail and towing a motor-boat, left St. John's harbour for Bay Roberts. She was manned by George C. Cave and his seventy-one-year-old father.

They were just outside the narrows when it began to blow hard from the southwest, and in no time a gale and mountainous seas began to batter the ship.

Just off from Sugar Loaf the mainmast broke and left the ship drifting before the gale. The *Hope* had no stern sails and she drifted down the coast at the mercy of the wind and tide. She was about seven miles offshore from Cape St. Francis when their motorboat broke her towline.

Recalling it recently in his home on Amherst Heights, ninety-one-year-old George Cave says, "There was quite a sea on, but we jibbed her and got her around to pick up the motorboat. We run her down until the two of us come together, and for a while we were afraid we were going to cut her in two, but Father put out his hand and just caught the boat, which stopped her headway a little until we fastened a rope to her."

They hauled the ship on course again as best they could, fighting for hours to keep her afloat, but the *Hope* was taking a fearful beating and seemed ready to founder. Said the old man to his son, "Well George, what are we going to do?"

Said George, "Sir, there's only one thing left to do, and that's leave her now and try and get to the Cape by motorboat."

His father was dubious. "The motorboat don't live that can get to shore in this wind."

Said George, "She'll live to go in if I'm aboard it!"

They hauled the motorboat alongside, and, after much manoeuvring, George got in first, then helped his father down and they started for shore. The *Hope* disappeared in the raging seas and was never seen again.

With the seas breaking over her bows, the motorboat pointed for the Cape. The first big sea broke over her coupling board, filled the old man's long rubbers, and nearly filled the boat. George Cave bailed desperately, afraid the engine batteries would give out. Three times the sea filled the boat, and each time furious bailing kept her afloat. It took them two hours to reach the Cape.

George Cave and his father were greeted by about twenty men at the Cape, and they discovered that the sudden storm had torn out all communications to the city.

They spent the night with the lightkeeper, and, the next morning, although it was still blowing a gale, they left for their home in Bay Roberts. But rounding Cripple Rock their boat sprang a leak, and it was decided that they should go into Bauline. However,

George pried the oakum from the ceiling of the cuddy and cinched the inside seams, effectively stopping the leak. But they had to spend the night in Portugal Cove.

The following day was Saturday, and George and his father made it safely to Bay Roberts that morning about eleven o'clock. It had taken them three days to get from St. John's to Bay Roberts and they had lost everything — their ship, 100 quintals of fish they had on board, their clothing, traps, and moorings.

This great storm cured George Cave of going to sea again, except for the occasional trip as a passenger on a large ship. His father stayed ashore after that, too, doing shoe repairs while George went to work with Captain John Parsons.

Of course the ship, and fishing, was a side business with the Caves. George's father was the first local shoemaker in Bay Roberts and George had worked with him from the time he was a small boy, but his dad liked the sea and always owned a ship of some kind.

George Cave lived and worked in Boston for six years after that terrible time at sea. Then he came home and opened a shoe repair store in Bay Roberts. He worked at it until he was eighty years old.

The EMPRESS OF SCOTLAND

CAPTAIN JOHN WALLACE THOMAS

During World War II, Captain John Wallace Thomas, CBE, was the famous captain of a famous ship, the *Empress of Scotland*, formerly the *Empress of Japan*, and he won the decoration Commander of the British Empire for masterful handling of the *Empress of Scotland* when the big liner was attacked by enemy aircraft off the northern coast of Ireland in 1940.

Captain Thomas, a Newfoundlander, was born in Harbour le Cou. He took to the sea when he was fourteen and fished off the Grand Banks and the Rose Blanche Banks until he was twenty-three. Says his widow, Mrs. Anne Thomas, "If anyone asked him how long he'd been at sea, he'd say, 'Since I was two.'"

In his letters Captain Thomas said, "We fished during the winter on the Banks and during the summer we traded between Sydney, Nova Scotia, and Prince Edward Island in our schooner, and of course we did a little smuggling as there was heavy duty on things such as shoes, sugar and other things into Newfoundland."

Let it be known that smuggling was not considered criminal by the fishermen in those days; it was merely a matter of having only so much money with which to clothe and feed their families. It was also a matter of the downtrodden fishermen getting the better of those "towny officials," those "know-it-alls." Shoes and sugar were the commodities smuggled past the officious "smarties" from St. John's.

Captain Thomas was destined for better things than fishing and smuggling for the necessities of life. In 1910, at the age of twenty-three years he left Newfoundland for Vancouver, British Columbia, Canada.

Mrs. Thomas recounts, "I think that my husband almost pioneered all of the Newfoundlanders that came out to Vancouver form Harbour le Cou—there's quite a crowd of them out there. He was rather ambitious and I think he found the little outport confining. He rather resented the lack of things; the lack of education, and he had to get it."

Captain Thomas left Harbour le Cou for good and, Mrs. Thomas says, he joined the National Steamship Company.

The next few years found Captain Thomas sailing coastwise out of Vancouver, and, in his spare time, he learned navigation and won his coast mate's ticket. He wound up as Third Officer on a freighter bound for England.

At the outbreak of World War I, John Wallace Thomas tried to enlist in the army and navy, but both services were slow in making up their minds to take him, so he stayed with the merchant marine.

At this time, he was the Third Officer on the *Minabrae,* a Air Naval oil tanker attached to the fleet at Scapa Flow, where the Battle of Jutland took place. The tanker was oiling the battle cruiser *Revenge* a few hundred miles off Gibraltar when word came that the German fleet was out. "That's a sight no one can forget seeing, the fleet forming up in battle formation and proceeding to sea," wrote Captain Thomas.

Another time, on the ship *Meroe* when Captain Thomas was a young officer, the ship was torpedoed, and sinking, and John Thomas had his boat lowered and ready to pull away when someone discovered the cook was missing. John ran back to the galley and found the cook (who was deaf as a gatepost) whistling merrily away, unaware that the ship had been torpedoed and was sinking!

With the cook safely aboard the lifeboat they pulled away, when another seaman noticed the Old Man was still on the bridge. The captain was seventy years old and quite determined to go down with his ship, so back to the sinking ship they rowed and John Thomas made his way to the bridge, where he had to do some fast talking to persuade the Old Man to leave the ship.

He wrote, "I had to lower the old boy down the side of the ship, for which my hands suffered badly from rope burns."

Canadian Pacific records that Captain John Thomas entered into its service November 24, 1916, serving in various capacities in the *Empress of Asia, Empress of Russia, Empress of Canada, Empress of France,* and latterly, in the *Empress of Scotland.*

He was given command of the troopship *Empress of Scotland* in July of 1940, and ship and man were together for the next eight and a half years. He had a short voyage for his first in the top job. The day he took over he sailed her from Hong Kong to Manila, arriving there with a load of evacuees only two days later.

It was November 9, 1940, when his ship, one day out of Glasgow and about 400 miles west of Ireland, was attacked by enemy aircraft.

The attack took place at 9:15 A.M., just two weeks after the *Empress of Britain* had been fatally hit in about the same position. Enemy aircraft dropped bombs and raked the big ship with machine-gun fire. Bombs dropped on the starboard and port sides of the ship, splintering everything movable in the cabins.

One bomb scored a hit on the port side and the ship was lifted out of the water stern-first. It felt as if the ship had broken amidships, but she hadn't, and, in a few minutes, had recovered, when another bomb struck the ship aft, hitting the railing and falling into the sea.

Meanwhile, Captain Thomas manoeuvred the ship, giving orders to his Chinese quartermaster, Ho Kan, to zigzag so that when the bombs fell the *Empress* was no longer there.

But the *Empress* was crippled by the bomb that struck aft and fell into the sea. Captain Thomas recalled during an interview some eighteen years after the incident, "It burst below, took off part of the rudder, and started glands and valves in the engine room. The explosion smashed the shaft bearings, and it was thanks to an engine-room gang posted in the shaft tunnel to oil the bearings with buckets that we were able to make port. The water intakes were cracked, too, and were wired together to get sufficient water.

"The six-inch gun was thrown off its bed by the shock of the 'near-miss,' and every switch in the engine room was thrown off. Passengers, mainly women and children from the Far East, behaved excellently."

Captain John Wallace Thomas received the highest decoration earned by any Canadian Pacific ship-master in the merchant service during the war: the Commander of the Order of the British Empire (CBE), awarded for the handling of *The Empress of Scotland* while under attack by enemy aircraft, November 9, 1940.

His quartermaster, Ho Kan, was awarded the British Empire Medal on Captain Thomas's recommendation.

It is recorded that Ho Kan came to Captain Thomas when he received notification of the award. "I got letter from King," he stated.

Said John Thomas, "What for?"

Replied Ho Kan, "Me no go to see King, I speak no English."

Said Captain Thomas, "The King no speak Chinese!"

The *Empress* returned to Belfast, Ireland, for repairs and a few months later continued her war service, still under the command of "Big Jack," as Captain Thomas was known.

The *Empress* and "Big Jack" Thomas were in Singapore, January 1942, that critical period after the fall of Hong Kong. During her three days in the harbour of Singapore the causeway to the mainland had been demolished and the liner was under almost constant aerial attack. Said Captain Thomas, "We were under attack for three days and nights, but they missed us by feet, with only structural damage." One bomb fell on the wharf beside the ship, setting fire to piles of coal and rubber.

The *Empress* had to evacuate 1,700 woman and children, and Captain Thomas recalled, "With the wharf ablaze we had to get anything that floated and embark them from the water side, with many of them crawling through port holes. By this time, *Tojo* was down on the Johore Peninsula only a few miles away. Why they let us escape is a mystery to me."

The *Empress* logged 478,761 miles during the actual war years and carried 219,185 military personnel, but with civilians, prisoners-of-war, and other natives, carried a grand total of 258,192.

Not only was Captain Thomas never relieved during his tenure of command, July 1940 to the end of hostilities, he was continuously aboard the ship from the outbreak of the war, when he was staff captain — a record unequalled throughout the whole Canadian Pacific Fleet.

As Canadian Pacific puts it, "The real record for *Empress of Scotland*, regardless of her astronomical mileage figures and such statistics, lay in the smallest statistic in her record: 'Captains, *one*.'"

Captain John Wallace Thomas was retired January 1, 1949, and he lived in Vancouver with his wife and son, Dr. John Philip Thomas. He was asked how he had felt about retirement, and replied, "King George asked me the same question. I couldn't tell him."

"Big Jack" Thomas made good copy for some of Canada's foremost writers who were always trying to interview him, but for the most part he was not partial to publicity.

One such article says that Captain Thomas was decorated three times, but "Big Jack" would never discuss it, not with the press or his family. He wasn't interested in discussing it at all, said Mrs. Thomas. "He's got a half-dozen medals, but in all the years at home I've never heard him discuss it. It was a matter that was finished and he was glad that it was finished. It was done. He did his duty and that was all there was to it."

"Big Jack" Thomas was a man who knew what he wanted and was bound to get it. While on a voyage to Liverpool, England, during the First World War, he was introduced to a tiny, lovely English girl through a seaman friend she was dating, and, as she recalls it, the big, quiet man had little or nothing to say and she wasn't particularly impressed. He astounded her by turning up at her church one night and sitting beside her. Afterwards she thought, *What on earth am I going to do with this man*?

The safest thing was to invite him home for a cup of coffee, which she did, and every trip after that he came to see her, and after six months told her that she was going back to Canada with him.

"Never!" she replied, unable to see herself living anywhere but in Liverpool.

He replied, "Oh, yes you are!"

She did, and never regretted it. "He was a wonderful man. We had forty-six wonderful years together, and the last seventeen since he retired were the happiest of them all."

Captain Thomas received his English Master's ticket (the highest in the world) in Liverpool. He passed so highly the examiner wanted him to sit for his extra master's ticket the next week, but the ship was sailing and there was no time.

"He was so quiet, you never knew if he was serious or not. He was always joking," Mrs. Thomas said.

Captain John Wallace Thomas died in his sleep July 24, 1965. Besides his wife, he left a son, Dr. John Philip Thomas, a blood specialist at the Vancouver General Hospital, and had four grandchildren.

Newfoundland may have been unaware that this son was doing her proud during those turbulent years, but Canada was very much aware of Captain John Wallace Thomas.

Meantime, the old *Empress of Scotland* carried on. The Canadian Pacific sold her on January 17, 1958, to Hamburg–Atlantic Line GMBH and Co., Hamburg, Germany. She was remodelled to carry 1,200 passengers on a regular service for the Hamburg–Atlantic Line, on the North Atlantic between New York and ports in Britain, France, and Germany.

NEWFOUNDLANDERS ALL

The Thomas name is an illustrious one in the shipping circles of the west coast of Canada. The three Thomas brothers, Captain John "Big Jack," Captain Arthur, and Captain William Thomas settled in Vancouver after they left Harbour le Cou, Newfoundland, and proceeded to make the Thomas name one to be highly respected.

CAPTAIN ARTHUR THOMAS

In a letter, Captain Arthur Thomas is remembered by "Big Jack." "I never mentioned Arthur before. He was master of a Canadian government vessel during the war. He also took a deep-sea tug from Vancouver to England in 1943 and, after the war, he was in command of a deep-sea tug on the Pacific and towed in many damaged ships. His was the *big* job."

In 1948, Captain Arthur Thomas was in command of the SS *Salvage King*, the most powerful tug on the Pacific coast. He served with the Pacific Salvage Company for many years. It was the old *Salvage King* that he delivered to the British Admiralty in England, 1943.

CAPTAIN WILLIAM THOMAS

Captain William Thomas, the youngest of the seafaring brothers, also showed the same daring and bravery when nature was on the rampage. This story also took place during the war years, when the U.S. Army transport *Kvichak* grounded one stormy January night on Finlayson Inlet, 150 miles south of Prince Rupert, British Columbia.

Giant waves battered the wrecked ship, and three lifeboats filled with survivors made it to a rocky island about 500 yards from the *Kvichak*.

Captain William Thomas was the master of the American Can Company vessel *Cancolim* from Vancouver, and she dared the heavy seas and dangerous rocks to remove the boatloads of shipwreck victims from the island.

Once, during the rescue process, the *Cancolim* ran aground but worked herself free, continuing to rescue the survivors in storm-tossed waters.

Of the three brothers, William was the last survivor and lived on Vancouver island.

Newfoundland can be very proud of her captains courageous!

John Cabot Landed in Torbay?

Treasure trove...pirates' gold...headless ghosts. Does that send you into guffaws of laughter? What about Cabot landing in Torbay? More laughter?

Well, laugh away, but remember there are all kinds of treasure, and if you have an ounce of adventure in your bones, or an insatiable curiosity about things not of this era, you would get as interested as I did when some "treasures" came to light recently at Torbay. It would send you sniffing into the wind like a hound on the trail of game.

Torbay had long been noted for its legends of buried treasure and the headless ghost that guards the treasure, and also for its historical past. The legends of buried treasure the majority of us take with a grain of salt, but there are many kinds of buried treasure, and when one such treasure was brought to my attention recently by Torbay fisherman and prospector Jack Dodd, we decided to have a look and possibly take a picture or two.

Jack Dodd had been digging for worms on one of the lonely hills of Torbay and had unearthed a "breast hook" of the type used by ships three or more hundred years ago. He had been digging on the edge of a cliff where water seeped from a spring somewhere deep within the bowels of the hills. Having found the hook he dug further, forgetting the worms, and unearthed a solidly built square wooden drain made of some type of "foreign" wood.

Sihouette of a bleached apple tree on the McCarthy property.

So, on his next trip to the city for supplies, Mr. Dodd dropped these enticing bits of information across our desks, asserting that no one living in Torbay today knew the existence of such a drain, and that, furthermore, *the cold clear water ran down over the cliff into Treasure Cove.*

Well! Everyone knows that Treasure Cove was the landing spot for pirates centuries ago, and everyone knows that Treasure Cove is haunted by a headless man and a dog with large, fiery eyes, guarding buried treasure, and that when they walk the beach at the witching hour the rattle of chains is like the roar of thunder.

Of course, this is seen and heard only by those who dare to approach the cove at the witching hour, and no one has been brave enough to do so in this century, it seems, because the last two men who dared were never the same. One died mysteriously a year later and the other took to his bed and never walked again. He is remembered by some people of Torbay today.

So, with this chilling bit of evidence, Cassie Brown and photographer Frank Kennedy decided we weren't really interested in that kind of treasure guarded by ghosts, but that wooden drain was most intriguing. Besides, it was broad daylight!

So, that same day we took Jack Dodd back to Torbay with his supplies we examined the rusted "breast hook," which is not in use on today's modern ships but of the type used on square-riggers and ships of another era.

Jack Dodd carefully pointed out that the hook was cast all in one piece (something not done in this day and age). I was seeing in my mind's eye pirate ships, skull and crossbones, and the distinct rigging of a galleon...

But on to that drain, made of some "foreign" wood. We had to tramp the hills to reach that. We could only go so far by car, Treasure Cove and the drain being along the hill "a piece."

Naturally we were not clad for hill climbing, this female's feet ensconced in high-heeled shoes, but...ah, well!

Slipping, sliding, teetering wildly on icy ledges, we crossed a makeshift road spanning a river. Only a clump of grass here, and a rock there protruding from the ice, saved us from sliding off the road into the river below, but we made it to the comparative safety of the ice-crusted hill.

First we had to see the "pirate well," chiselled by hand out of solid rock centuries ago. This well, just feet from the sea, had obviously been chiselled by hand. It is supposedly hundreds of years old, and legend has it that it is a marker for the buried treasure in Treasure Cove "along the shore a piece."

Legend also has it that some of the treasure was actually discovered by one man a couple of hundred years back, a lonely, mysterious man who claimed, during bouts of drinking, that he had put it back because "it wasn't his."

So much for the pirate's well and on to Treasure Cove, "along a ways." Slipping and sliding, we reached a rocky bluff that jutted out into the sea and gazed down into a peaceful little cove where one would like to have a nice picnic some summer day.

Right now the cove was calm and peaceful and the tide was low, but above the high-water mark frozen spray coated the cliffs. On the far side were the remains of an abandoned stage, still usable, according to Jack Dodd, but, with spidery legs and a generally dilapidated condition, it looked ready to collapse in the first gentle breeze.

Our particular treasure trove was on the far side of Treasure Cove, so we made our careful way up the hill, across the top, and down the far side—to the edge of the cliff.

There it was, the snout of the wooden drain, exposed for the first time in centuries. (At least it was exciting to think in terms of centuries.) Black, it looked perfectly square and solidly put together.

The crystal clear water flowed out of it and down over the cliff into the cove. "This," said Jack Dodd, "might have been placed here by pirates for drinking water. The wood in this drain is not Newfoundland wood. It's been there a long time and has been preserved by the type of clay around it."

Well now, it had to be put there by someone, and why not pirates? In this present day and age there seemed to be no rhyme or reason for such a well-constructed drain on the isolated hills of Torbay—and it did drain into the legendary Treasure Cove, now, didn't it?

Balancing against the extreme edge of the cliff, Frank Kennedy braced himself and took a picture or two. We could almost hear the ghostly pirate turning over in his grave.

Before leaving we did get a few pieces of wood for the Department of Mines and Resources to play around with.

While it was nippy, it was a beautiful day, and Mr. Dodd poured into our receptive ears tales of the legendary pirates who moored their treasure-laden ships less than a thousand yards from the spot on which we were standing. "Just off there they used to moor their ships, it's said...then they would row into the cove there," he said.

He painted a vivid picture of the legendary ghost, a young boy, still wet behind the ears, and of his dog, who were selected by the pirate captain to "guard" the treasure.

The boy discovered that he had "volunteered," and, on the very beach of Treasure Cove, met an untimely end when they severed his head from his body. His dog, with a ferocious roar, jumped for the throat of the killer, but the brave animal was quickly "done in" — hence the headless ghost and the dog with the fiery eyes.

"Nobody," said Mr. Dodd solemnly, "will be found near Treasure Cove after dark."

He turned to me. "While you're down here you should take a look at that old apple tree I was telling you about."

Last fall he had told me a story about an apple tree brought from Ireland in the sixteenth century, and still standing in Torbay. Dead of course, but still standing.

"Is it far?"

"About five minutes' walk," says he.

A good five minutes it was, over "the road along the shore" as it was called, when it should have been called "the road along the cliffs!"

Certain parts of the road had been eaten away and, on a dark night, anyone daring to traverse it could walk right off the cliff into the sea.

But on to the apple tree.

The very first settler in Torbay was a Dennis McCarthy, a cooper. For ten years he remained the only settler. Meantime, he married an Irish lass, and one year she went back to Ireland to visit her parents. When she returned she carried a seedling apple tree and planted it high on the hill near their home.

The apple tree flourished and was still going strong when the McCarthy's passed from the scene. It is still standing today, hundreds of years later, bleached and silvered by the elements, just twenty to thirty feet from the spot where the McCarthy house had stood. This could be a historical treasure.

Sure enough, there it stood, its silvered limbs mutely pointing skyward. Nearby, a shallow depression and a vague outline was all that was left of the McCarthy house, where a man could wet his whistle on a good glass of rum for two cents.

We stood on the hill in the crisp, clean air, trying to visualize life as it was in the sixteenth century. The waters of the bay were flat and calm and the usual bustle of modern living was non-existent here. It didn't take too much concentration to see square-riggers riding at anchor or men and women in period costume.

But we had no further excuse to dally and so ended a pleasant and mildly exciting treasure hunt on the hills of Torbay.

But our treasure hunt wasn't to end there, for Jack Dodd, hot on the trail of the treasure trove, turned up a few days later with a couple of pieces of metal, silvery in colour but extremely light.

In spite of one's fondest hopes, it was not silver, but an alloy of some sort, although at the government lab,

Jack Dodd points to an ancient water drain.

technicians had not definitely decided what it contained. This, says Dodd, he found in the wooden drain.

But by far the most fascinating treasure trove was a stone "foot" imbedded in the earth near the drain, encased in "rock flour," a substance that accumulated in the ground around the rock, hardening and encasing the foot. Most interesting of all were the markings that came to light when the rock flour was chipped away.

The stone was of sandstone, not native to Torbay, and with the date 1497 scratched into the surface. Other markings indicated the name "Matthew." There was the flag of St. George and the CABT and other letters.

Naturally, our imaginations ran high, wide, and handsome.

Speculation was rife. Technicians were interested, *but*—what did the stone indicate? Surely not that Cabot landed in Torbay? It is simpler to suppose that some schoolboy, dreaming of the adventurous Cabot, had at one time scratched the date and name of the ship into the rock, as well as other hieroglyphics

Except, it is difficult to visualize a schoolboy retaining enough interest in ancient history to scratch dates and names on a rock.

Technicians agree that, in spite of the "rock flour," it is still difficult to determine the age of the markings on the stone, though they could easily be one hundred years old or five hundred.

So here our story of treasure ends with a drain, a few pieces of metal, a rusted breast hook, and a rock, the shape of a foot, with hieroglyphics. It also leaves us with the question. *Could* Cabot have landed in Torbay in 1497?

Well, why not?

And who knows? There may be buried treasure waiting to see the light of day.

There *could* be.

Cassie Brown...
The Writer

Floyd Spracklin

Editor's Note:

As a teacher, Floyd Spracklin was a committee
member of the Canada Council's Atlantic Region
National Book Festival Committee. This group
was responsible for funding library and school
visits from Canadian authors. The well-known
Newfoundland writer Cassie Brown was on his
list of potential presenters at G.C. Rowe. In the
spring of 1985 Cassie jumped at the opportunity
to visit Corner Brook and share her thoughts and
experiences with junior high students. One
evening, while at dinner, Floyd mentioned that
although the trip had been a success it was, albeit,
too short, and would she agree to putting more
thought and detail into a taped interview, based
on questions created by his writing students?
Cassie agreed. But, being the busy writer that she
was, she did not get around to committing herself
to this project until the following spring, only a
few short months before her death on December

30, 1986, at the age of sixty-seven. Cassie, ever the thorough and inquisitive person, spent hours either sitting down or pacing back and forth in her study with the list of student-generated questions and recording her responses on a tape recorder in her own home. That tape has been played many, many times for Floyd's writing students. It became a source of inspiration.

The Interview

WILL YOU TELL US A LITTLE ABOUT YOUR BIOGRAPHICAL BACKGROUND?

I WAS BORN IN ROSE BLANCHE and, well, I'm not going to be shy about it. I was born back in 1919, and it's not that I'm shy about it. I simply really do not discuss it, and don't ask me why...it's some little thing that we women have. So, I was born back in Rose Blanche, and of course I thought the sun rose and set in Rose Blanche. It was the place to be, and this is why [for] so many people who are born in the outport it is the be-all and end-all of their existence. It's only when you move away from a little place like Rose Blanche that you suddenly realize that there is a great big world out there. And it's just waiting for you, and you are waiting for it. Although you don't realize it at the time.

There were quite a few adventures in Rose Blanche. I fell through the ice, which I feel was a preparation for what I had to write about in my later years. Be that as it may, I fell through the ice, right through a hole. Well, I was only three years of age at the time. Needless to say it was not my fault, but the two young ladies who were taking me for a walk across the harbour kept their heads, and so here I am.

There was another time I fell in the harbour. I had slipped down to the wharf, which I should not have done because we had been forbidden to do that. My mother naturally was always quite worried about whether we went to the wharf. We would never survive, as the water was quite deep. I was quite curious, and guess what? I fell into twenty-five feet of water. And nearly drowned. I was saved only because some fishermen [were] working upon the wharf. Not one of them could swim, which seems to be pretty usual for fishermen around Newfoundland. Anyway, these fishermen saved me by forming a human chain and jumping into the harbour, into the water, and pulling me ashore.

So, you see, I've had a few close calls. I wrote about another one, in "Black Rock Sunker," entered in the Arts and Letters Competition. The entire story isn't true but is based on a true story our whole family was caught up in at the time. We were all in the boat and drifting up on Black Rock Sunker. If I recall correctly, within the past ten years I read about a schooner or ship which ran up on Black Rock Sunker and was lost. So it's quite...very infamous, let's say.

Anyway, we moved to St. John's when I was about eleven, and so life was not as exciting, I might say, in that aspect of living.

HOW DID YOU START WRITING?

WELL, MY PARENTS WERE ALWAYS LAYING DOWN THE LAW. That children should be seen and not heard. That syndrome. And, as there was a large family of us, there were at that time five, six, eventually eight of us altogether; there was probably good reason for them to make us all remain quiet and well behaved in the home. My mother had been a schoolteacher before she was married and to me she always was a schoolteacher. She was not the type that you become overly familiar with. You did not impose or impinge upon her space, and she was always like the stately, dignified queen, and so when she stated, "Children should be seen and not heard," you were seen and you were not heard. Consequently, all of us grew up quite well behaved and obedient, but you could never express your feelings.

So what I would do, and this is how I started writing...what I would do if I was annoyed or angry or anything...if anything had put me in a snit, let us say, I could not go to my mother and complain bitterly about what my sister did to me. You just did not do that at all. What I would do is I would take a pencil and a little scrap of paper and I would write down on this scrap of paper how annoyed I was, or that I didn't like so-and-so, or so-and-so had pushed me, someone had dug an elbow into my side. When there was something nice to say, I could not go to my mother or father with that, so I would also express it on a little piece of paper and a pencil, and that is how I started writing.

And it went on from there. I started...I would say I was about thirteen. It was one winter...we were in St. John's.

I began to write a novel, and I was quite caught up in it. I would sit there at the table with my books in front of me and write for hours. I was totally caught up in it and in the characters. I just loved them. My mother, incidentally, thought I was doing my homework. I really did not enjoy doing homework. It impinged

upon what free time I had, and yet it was very important, in looking back upon it now. It was very important. But anyway, I spent the whole winter writing,
and my mother was delighted. She simply thought I
was doing my homework, and I did not tell her the difference.

So...that was my first serious writing. Now, I wrote
a whole book, but when you're thirteen, one did not
really know enough about love or being in love to write
about it. So, consequently, I kind of got caught up and
lost in what I was writing. Nevertheless, I did finish the
book. Now, in the meantime, I suppose I should say
thank goodness—although I would like to be able to
lay my hands on it—we did move a couple of times,
and somehow or another that manuscript disappeared.
Thank goodness.

I continued writing. I joined the Hiking Club
when I was in my teens. I'm sure you have never
heard of the Hiking Club, because it had been started in the thirties. To join you had to be invited to
become a member...then you had to walk forty miles
in one day. That was the initiation into the
Newfoundland Hiking Club. Well, I did it. And I did
it well. I wound up with only one small blister on
my little left toe. But that one tiny blister could easily have been a hundred blisters on each foot, it was
that painful. I used to write these articles about hiking, and the sports editor of *The Daily News*, who
had a brother in the Hiking Club, used to pop down
and visit every now and again. He learned that I was
writing articles and asked would I send some of
them in to *The Daily News* for them to publish. Sort

of publicity for the Hiking Club. I was thrilled. Mind you, I never got a cent for it. But I was "published." That continued for a few years, and I continued to write long after the Hiking Club. Eventually, you know, we became "richer," let us say, and we didn't have to walk anywhere. And we all got cars...well, the Hiking Club folded after struggling along for a few years.

But, I was still writing. I married and had a son and a daughter and for a few years dropped the writing, but you know, it is *always there*. *It is always there!* It kind of nags at you, to pick it up and keep going. Consequently, I began to pick up writing again. And I entered some contests, weekly stories, contests on Radio Station CJON. I won quite frequently, but of course there was no money for the winners. But, you know, how wonderful it was to write and to win, the winners being chosen by the announcers at the radio station who read them. Being young and right up to the mark on what was what, and what they were interested in, I won every week. Finally, after thirteen weeks, all of the stories were taken and sent to Memorial University, and guess who won? Not me! But Ted Russell, who later became very famous as "Uncle Mose." So I had very good competition there. Then I began to do some writing for CBC Radio, which opened up a little bit more. And so it went. It just goes on. It picks up, and improves, and it enlarges and expands. And the next thing, before you know it, there I was also writing for the Department of Education in their School Broadcasts.

WHAT REALLY INSPIRED YOU TO BECOME A PUBLISHED AUTHOR?

I WROTE WHAT I WROTE and when I wrote because I *had* to write. There was no planning or anything. I didn't plan to be a writer, but all of those characters suddenly sort of appeared to me. They were suddenly before my eyes. And there they were doing their thing. And for a while I thought that I was the creator all of these characters. I thought that I was manipulating them, that I was plotting the story and that I would want these characters to do this and that I would want them to say that, and I would want them to become involved in this kind of action. It seems to me that, for a little while, these characters, ohhh, they were very cunning and very sly because they *did* what I wanted them to do, and that snared me. They got me into a trap. Now, if this sounds strange to you, well, you're not a writer. But if you do any amount of writing, I'm sure you have learned by now that you are simply the "objective reporter," and that these characters, they have come to you. They have a story to tell, and *you* are chosen to write their story.

Now, when this finally happened to me, I understood that I wasn't creating these characters, that they were already there. They had their own *being-ness*. They had their own reasons for being. If they were in a world that was different from mine, it did not matter. They had chosen me to write their story. And once I realized that, I think that my writing became more real and more vivid. But it took me a few years to get this kind of understanding, and consequently I was writing and writing and writing like you would never believe. And publishing, being a published author, never entered into my mind. It did not enter into my mind to write a book, perhaps because we were so far away and so isolated from the rest of the world. Almost still pre-Confederation, you might say, sort of out of sight of all these things.

If I didn't write about them, these characters, my mind, my brain, would probably have exploded because there would be more characters coming in. Until I had written their story and let them go on and do whatever it was they wanted me to do, once that certain story had been told, they could go on. They were satisfied. And others were "waiting in the wings," you could say. Simply waiting for me to give them my attention. I do say that the idea of becoming a published author did come to me, vaguely, in a sneaky sort of way, back in the early fifties when I was writing for CBC radio.

I had to give up writing romantic fiction, simply because it made the announcer laugh whenever he came to the boy/girl stories. The technician—on the other side of the glass in the studio, and facing the narrator—every time the boy/girl romantic end came into it, light as it was, the radio technician would make faces and go "kissy-kissy," "lovey-lovey." The narrator, John Murphy, now mayor of St. John's, said, "I have a helluva time to keep from laughing, so can you cut out the 'love stuff'?"

And that is what I did. And that is where my first book was born, because then I started looking for true Newfoundland stories. Mind you, a lot of the stories that I had been writing were based on my own experiences, but all the romantics were simply fiction. What I didn't realize was that all the characters were coming in and making the story very real and wonderful and exciting for me to write. But I had to go and slant my writing to a documentary type of writing for this program. And in a book of Mr. Smallwood's [Newfoundland's first Premier] early books of Newfoundland there was a three- or four-paragraph story about the *Newfoundland* disaster which occurred in 1914. Having read it, I went to the library to do further research, and, when I read it, I really could not believe my eyes. I say this frequently: "It was like reading a movie." It was so fantastic and so dramatic and so unbelievable. Well now, right there and then, that is where an idea came to me. Gee, you know, what a marvellous book this would make! However, I did not think in terms right then of sitting down and writing a book, because I had two small children, a husband, a house, and there simply wasn't the time, particularly with the children. I would be working well into the nights and writing my stories for the CBC Radio and my plays and whatnot, and then again for the Department of Education.

WAS THERE A SINGLE PERSON WHO ENCOURAGED YOU TO WRITE?

I HAD NO CHOICE, or I don't know what would have happened to me. Now, I wasn't particularly influenced. I had been reading from about the time I was seven or eight, as soon as I could read. My father had lots of books when we were in the outport. I didn't particularly care for winter, so I used to read a lot. I think he had 200 to 300 books. I would say by the time I was eleven and we had moved to St. John's I had read three-quarters of them, at least. So I read Dickens and Thackeray, and Marie Corelli, whom I found very interesting, but no one in particular. I can't say that anyone encouraged me, because I was myself.

WHAT INSPIRED YOU TO WRITE ABOUT NEWFOUNDLAND?

BECAUSE I KNOW NEWFOUNDLAND, and I am a Newfoundlander, and I am part of Newfoundland. The sea is part of me as I am a part of it. And the rocks and the trees, and everything that is Newfoundland. I think that if you planted it inside of me, I couldn't feel more Newfoundland. There is a small Newfoundland growing inside of me.

WOULD YOU SAY SELF-MOTIVATION IS PREFERABLE TO MODELLING ONESELF AFTER ANOTHER WRITER?

WELL, THAT'S ANOTHER WRITER, that's not you. You have to be your own individualistic person and only you know what you think and how you think. Only you can write about what you think and who you are, and so on and so forth. So, forget the modelling-yourself-after-anyone-else bit. It's for the birds.

DO YOU FEEL PRIVILEGED OR GIFTED WITH CERTAIN TALENTS?

YES, YES, YES, YES, YES — *yes*! I am very privileged because of the gift of certain talents. And the certain talents, you only know a few of them through my writings. You may know more of them when my next book is published. And that's all I'm going to say about that.

WOULD YOU ELABORATE ON MENTAL IMAGES OR YOUR "LITTLE PEOPLE"?

WHEN I WAS GROWING UP I always had pictures of people and things and places in my mind. One of them was a picture of myself on an ocean liner. It was me because if I look in the mirror, I see a reflection of me. Therefore, this mental picture I had of me was a reflection of me, I suppose. And I was on an ocean liner. And, therefore, perhaps at that time, that sometime or another, I would be on an ocean liner. And in other aspects of my writing, for instance, let us take *Death on the Ice*.

I have spoken of mental images to many students. When I was writing *Death on the Ice* I would find myself like I was in a theatre, perhaps. I would be in a great big box looking down as though in a theatre, looking down upon the icefields — white and slowly moving, heaving up and down with the heavy groundswell. And I would see those little black figures of men going over the ice and I would watch them, and I was very remote from it. I was very detached. I would watch the scene before me, and I would see the snowstorm approaching. Then, suddenly — quite suddenly — I would no longer be detached and watching them. I would be totally involved, and I would be down on the ice right with them. And I would be walking along, slogging along with them and hearing the men talking and saying these things to each other, that there was going to be another disaster. And I was as cold, and I was as tired, and I was as chilled as *they* were. And, I was there. *I was there*! And that is all there is to it.

Now, I would become detached again, just observing, as if I were a big giant looking down upon a little theatre as from a great distance. And yet I could see everything quite clearly. And again, when it was necessary for me to experience what was going on, I would find myself right down there in the thick of it. And I would be as cold, and I would be as wet, and I would be as uncomfortable, and I would be as hungry as those men were. Now, that is what mental imagery is.

And as far as my "little people" are concerned, I didn't know anything about "little people" at all. Not until I had first started doing a story for radio about the sealing disaster, which was later *Death on the Ice*. It was as if those men had chosen *me* to write their story. Those men long dead and those men who were still alive. It was as if on another level they had decided that the time had come for their story to be told. And therefore, when I first began to research it for writing a story for radio, it was as if they grabbed hold to me, as if they said to each other, "We've got her!" In other words, they had my attention, because, from that moment on, they never left me alone. They just stayed with me and were with me and always kept the story of that disaster alive in my mind, very much alive in my mind. And as the time went on and the years went on, and my children were growing up and I was work-ing—as a newspaper reporter by this time—they never...they never left me alone. They would prod and nudge me for a little while, and they would make things come my way. Everything came my way, as you can tell by reading the book. So, these are my "little people," and when I have to tap into them today I just say to them, "Help me! I need help!!" It *works*! And it's lovely.

DO YOU SEE YOURSELF CHANNELLING YOUR INTERESTS IN SOME OTHER AREAS, OTHER THAN THE WRITING OF DISASTERS?

YOU BET YOUR BOOTS! I can't write any more disasters. It doesn't work for me anymore. When I say it doesn't work for me anymore, it's because I do not wish to become so totally involved, to take such a great length of time, to get into "death and disaster." I want to write other, happy, exciting, and dramatic things. My books have been "exciting and dramatic," and great sagas of the sea, but I want to write other things. And, so, I am. It's interesting that you should use the word "chan-nelling," because I am channelling my interests in anoth-er area which you, I am sure, will find very interesting. I do not feel comfortable interviewing survivors of dis-aster. I find myself getting very involved and wanting to put myself in their shoes. I've done that for fifteen years, and that is enough. *That is enough*! One has to be very careful about what one writes. And one has to be very sure that what one is writing is correct. And, therefore, it has to be "painstaking," and, uh, very *pains-taking*!

WHAT OF YOUR OTHER WRITINGS, OTHER THAN YOUR PUBLISHED BOOKS?

I HAVE WRITTEN FANTASY, and I've had radio plays, and documentaries on the CBC National Network. I love fantasy, incidentally, because what we call fantasy, I have another phrase for it. It is "other worldness," and it is as legitimate as the physical world, and I don't care what anyone says, it is quite legitimate. I think that my next book...you will totally understand what I am saying. Other than that, it's rather difficult to discuss it.

DO YOU SET DEADLINES WHEN YOU WRITE, APART FROM THOSE IMPOSED BY PUBLISHERS?

MY POOR PUBLISHERS. You know, they keep writing me letters. "How is your book coming?" They know about this one I am writing. They were hoping it was going to be another disaster, of course, and I simply told them— I was up there in May—and I said to my editor, "Well, I'm just not into that, and if you want to see what I am writing you are welcome to read it," and they said, "We will see. We will read anything that you write." So, I am now polishing that book. It is written but it needs polishing, and that is what I am doing. And so, therefore, I set myself a deadline, but the thing is, if it doesn't flow, it doesn't flow for a reason. And, therefore, I do not push it. I cannot push it. It will not happen. Nothing happens. So, I go with the flow. And to heck with the deadlines.

And if any publisher is interested in me, they too will have to say, "To heck with the deadlines!"

IT TOOK YOU FIVE YEARS TO WRITE EACH OF YOUR BOOKS. EXACTLY HOW MUCH TIME WAS INVOLVED ON A DAILY OR WEEKLY BASIS?

ONCE I GET INVOLVED IN A BOOK, IT JUST...again the flow, has...is very important. But once I get into it I have to keep going. With the books that required so much research and so much study, I had to take breaks from it. Go on a holiday or something. That I *can* do!

But in this kind of writing that I'm doing now, if I'm going on a holiday somewhere I will take my manuscript with me or take a copy of it. And I will work on it where I am, because it is so much a part of me. Just doing what other people do—driving and going and seeing places and things—it's fine. I love it. But my manuscript is so much a part of me that it must be there for me to pick up and do a little polishing in "spare" moments. So you might say that, really and truly, it is ongoing at all times and I am totally involved.

DOES WRITING A BOOK INTERFERE WITH YOUR PERSONAL OR FAMILY LIFE IN ANY MAJOR WAY?

YES! WELL, LET ME PUT IT THIS WAY. My family, they're around me at all times. I am around them. And I am writing, and they have accepted it. I think that if I didn't write and sat around and did nothing, that it would be upsetting to them because I would not be doing what I am supposed to be doing. So, it doesn't interfere in this respect.

I don't have a great social life because I am writing all the time, and the funny thing about it is that my writing life is more real than the social life. And, so, it has impinged a great deal, in that I cannot go out and just sit down and talk about the ordinary, everyday little things that women sit around and talk about. It's not a part of my life.

It's strange, and yet I feel totally out of my selfness, when I have to sit down and listen to people just chit-chatting about their personal lives, because the personal little things that go on in their lives *is* their life and it isn't *mine*.

DOES THE BOOK THAT YOU'RE WORKING ON BECOME YOUR LIFE OR PART OF IT?

WELL, YES, yes, yes. *Yes*, indeed. I live the book. The book is me. I am the book, and that is it.

WHICH NOVEL AT THIS MOMENT DO YOU HAVE A SPECIAL PREFERENCE FOR?

OF MY THREE BOOKS WHICH ARE DOCUMENTARIES, really, it's hard to say. *Death on the Ice*? I lived through it. It was my favourite. *A Winter's Tale*? I lived through it. I loved it. But, *Standing into Danger* was something else. I lived through it. It was so dramatic and so exciting that—I've said this probably a hundred times—I was in a constant state of excitement all the time that I was writing it. And that I was involved in it. I was a part of it. And I had met just enough of these survivors, about twenty-eight or thirty of them, to make it all the more realistic. All the more, all the more true, and yet "true" is not the correct word, but it just became *more* true when I got involved with it. And so, consequently, I feel that the *whole world* should read this book because the Newfoundlanders were so brave. The American sailors were so brave. They were so brave and so great, and the Newfoundlanders, all, you could hardly differentiate. So brave and so great. And so wonderful. All rising above themselves, so *Standing Into Danger*, perhaps [for] *Standing Into Danger* I do have a bit of a special preference.

AND HOW DOES IT FEEL TO BE A POPULAR WRITER?

WONDERFUL! I LOVE IT, and I hope to be even more popular. Sometimes I pick up these books and look at them in wonder and say, "Did I really.... Did I?" And I did. I did.

ARE YOU DISSATISFIED WITH EITHER OF YOUR BOOKS?

NO, I'M NOT DISSATISFIED. I'm not dissatisfied, and why or why not? I worked like a dog on those books, and how can I be dissatisfied with them? It's...it's the record of my existence, and I love it.

ARE YOU WRITING AT THE PRESENT TIME?

IT'S SO STRANGE THAT YOU SHOULD ASK THAT, because after *Standing Into Danger* I was unwell for quite a while. In fact, I was unwell when I was writing all of my books. But I was quite unwell in '79. And, uh '80 and '81. And having been in hospital in the intensive care for a considerable time, I want to live in the present instead of living as in the past, working with my nose to the grindstone. I want to live *now*. And so I decided to take a year's break. That year went by so fast! I took another year's break. Zip! Zip! It was gone even faster. So, coming up to '82 I was beginning to feel uneasy because I didn't want to settle down to writing another marine disaster. It was simply too demanding. I would be closeted in part of the house here for another five years. I wanted to write, and yet I remember saying one day I was in a school here in St. John's, with children from kindergarten to grade 5. The kindergarten children were lying on the carpet of the library, around my feet. If I wanted to move around I would have to step over them or walk very carefully among them. And it was delightful. It was so informal and everything, and so I would ask a question which was a yes or a no, and all of the children would reply "Yessss," or "Nooooooo." One of the older children got up and said to me, "Are you writing a book right now, Mrs. Brown?"

And I said, "No. I'm not. I'm taking a break."

And she said, "Are you going to write another book?"

I said, "I don't know. Right now I feel as if I do not want to write another book. I don't! I do not want to write another book. Do *you* think I should write another book if I don't want to?"

And all the children said, "Nnooooooo!"

One little, tiny voice from somewhere out there piped up and said, "Yessss!"

I said, "Out of the mouths of babes!"

I couldn't tell which one it was. There were probably thirty or forty or more there. But that one little voice...it was like my conscience saying to me, "You must write. You really *do* want to write." This dearest light and childish and beautiful voice piping up and saying, "Yesss!" Out of all the multitude of children there.

And, so, I *did* feel the need to write. I needed to write. I really needed to write. But, if everybody was expecting another marine disaster from me, they were *not* going to get it. I wanted to write something else. I didn't know what it was. I knew that I wanted to write something, perhaps a suspense mystery. I didn't want to write another documentary. But I couldn't get started on it. I would *not* get started on it. And then, this winter, *it* happened. And that's all I'm going to say about *that*. Wait until you read it.

WOULD YOU BE INTERESTED IN COMPILING A COLLECTION OF YOUR PREVIOUS WORK? SHORT STORIES AND SO FORTH?

NO, ABSOLUTELY NOT. That's finished. It's all behind me. Finished. And you don't go back. You only go forward.

DO YOU HAVE ANY REAL DESIRE TO SEE ONE OR MORE OF YOUR BOOKS ACCEPTED FOR PRODUCTION, MOVIE RIGHTS, ETC.?

YES. THERE HAVE BEEN SO MANY, SO MANY INQUIRES. Long-distance calls from other parts of Canada. Nothing has happened, of course, and I feel that nothing will happen until it has been decreed by the powers that be. In other words, when the time is right for it and the right script is written. I am sure that right script will not be written unless I write it. But, on the other hand, I don't want to become involved in it.

WHAT ARE YOUR VIEWS ON EDITORIAL PRIVILEGES AND CENSORSHIP?

EDITORIAL PRIVILEGE AND CENSORSHIP. What do I know about editorial privileges and censorship? Do I know *any*thing about editorial privileges and censorship? When I was working with the newspaper, and the editor took a story and did his thing with it, it didn't matter that much, because it was strictly news. In actuality they did not touch any of my material. They were pleased with what I gave them, and they just left it alone for the most part, except for the proofreader who got his hands on it and, sometimes in putting his spelling on it, messed everything up.

Censorship? Well, now that's something else. I personally feel that if a writer wishes to have his or her books in a school, for students, I think that the four-letter words are quite unnecessary. Students themselves learn the language on the streets. So, therefore, it's not necessary for them to get it from literature as well. In *Standing Into Danger*, in quoting one of the officers I interviewed, I did a couple of times use a four-letter word, and I was very uncomfortable. Yet, I felt I had to be true to what he was saying. I don't know what possessed me to put it in—they are not the worst words in the world—and yet I am not a four-letter-word user myself. So, when I abridged it I removed it all, because if it's ever going in the schools it is the abridged work in the paperback which will go in.

I really would not be comfortable if I knew that my own children when they were going to school were studying a book which had the four-letter words. I'm not a prude, mind you. And perhaps that's what I was proving when I put it in, when I put those couple of words in *Standing Into Danger*. Perhaps I had to prove that I wasn't a prude. I know they are simply words, but why—when it comes to the student body—teach students to keep their tongues in the gutter? So I removed them from the paper edition of *Standing Into Danger*, and I am more comfortable.

IS THERE A CAREER TO BE MADE FORM WRITING, AND, IF SO, WHAT SPECIAL TRAINING WOULD YOU RECOMMEND?

HAVEN'T YOU BEEN READING ALL THE MAGAZINE ARTICLES? Doesn't it state in all the articles that authors and writers are among the poorest of the poor? That their literary achievements will not keep the "wolf from the door"? Unless you are a Harold Robbins writer, who's really into that dicey little area...pornography, in a way.

Pornography, yes, sort of, although they call it litera- ture, and which after a while becomes very boring to read.

I can only quote Ted Russell. When Ted suddenly came on the scene, Ted and his wife, Dora, used to come out here to Karwood Kabins quite a bit. We knew them quite well. When he suddenly became so much in demand — his writings were so popular — I thought that he was going to make a career of it. And I asked him. I said, "Now, Ted, are you going to make a career of writing?"

And he said, "Cassie, I can make three-quarters of a living from my writing, but three-quarters of a living is not enough." And that is what Ted Russell said to me in the house when he was visiting us one evening.

And so, I would say that if the bread on the table and the clothing on my back and the roof over my head had to come from my writing income, well, I would not make it. Bearing in mind that I have just three books on the market. All three, mind you, still sell. But, you know, there's not a "crush and rush" sell. It's not like the thousands or the millions of dollars are rolling in, although I would say that what I am getting from roy- alties is much more than the average writer is getting. I probably get more. But, I wouldn't say either that I have been paid for the amount of time and effort that went into the production of those books.

You would have to have no responsibilities if you wanted to make a career from writing. You would have to have no family to look after, no rent to pay, no responsibilities. Let's just put it that way. But there's a career in the newspaper field. Of course there are some who make a career of writing, but I'm a member of the Author's Guild of America, the Writer's League of America, and they are always looking for grants, always looking for money to exist on as they write their books. A lot of these greatly established writers are not making a big plush living from it. I wouldn't say so, particularly here in Newfoundland.

I never had any special training myself. The young student should study his English, get a good working knowledge of grammar. If he has that, a good working knowledge of grammar, that's half the battle. He doesn't need to be a "sloppy gar!" A surprising number of writers who had this great urge to write don't have a good grounding, so their work is a little bit on the sloppy side—careless. And no editor has the time to wade through work that's sloppy and careless.

And of course, have the ideas to put together, but trust more to those inner characters that come to the fore. So, what advice do I have for young writers? Write, write, write, write, keep writing, and don't model yourself after anybody else. Just do your own thing.

There was a young man in here about two hours ago. He has one more semester to go at the university to get his degree in English, and he *wants to write*. And he asked me, "What do you recommend?" He had about thirty pieces. "Now, what could be done to improve them?" I would only suggest to him that he take his own work, get a good national magazine, and compare them. Take paragraph one of this very professional writer and compare it with his own paragraph form. See how many redundancies he has there, how many unnecessary adjectives. And if he can take a sentence or two or a paragraph and cut out everything that's unnecessary and have the pure gem of what he is saying. So, if they can say what they said, in one sentence, that may be a very great help.

Other than that, I would say to them, "Just write and keep on writing. And write, and write, and write, and write, and write, and write, and write."

SOURCES: PART ONE

1. "Rose Blanche and Me" *The Book Of Newfoundland, Vol. 6.* Newfoundland Book Publishers. pp. 465–472.

SOURCES: PART TWO (*THE DAILY NEWS*)

1. "The *Caribou* was Struck Down." October 16, 1964

2. "Death March: The Story of a Sealing Disaster." March 31, 1964.

3. "Death March: Survived Because He was in Love." Cecil Mouland's story. October 27, 1964.

4. "Death March: Survivor Wesley Collins Recalls Days of Disaster." March 31, 1964.

5. The *Florizel* Disaster Forty-Five Years Ago." March 6, 1963.

6. The *Florizel*: Kitty Cantwell's Story. "Disaster Cured Urge To Travel." February 23, 1965.

7. "A Tragedy at St. Jacques Island." Katherine Fiander's Story, January 8, 1965.

8. "Captain Disallows Abandoning Ship, Sealing Crew Mutiny On S.S. *Diana*." March 12, 1965.

9. "The *Leicester*: Saved from the Sea by Newfoundlanders." November 1, 1965.

10. "Oldtimer Recalls Loss of the *Hope*." November 24, 1965

11. "The Famous Captain of a Famous Ship." Captain John Thomas and *The Empress of Scotland*. February 1, 1966.

12. "Treasures of Torbay." February 7, 1963.

SOURCES: PART THREE

1. Spracklin, Floyd. Taped responses by Cassie Brown, to questions created by writing students at G.C. Rowe Junior High School, Corner Brook, 1985.